Keynesian Economics:

The Search for First Principles

By the same author

Theories of the Bargaining Process, George Allen & Unwin, 1968.

Keynesian Economics:

The Search for First Principles

ALAN CODDINGTON
Queen Mary College, University of London

London
GEORGE ALLEN & UNWIN
Boston   Sydney

George Allen & Unwin (Publishers) Ltd,
40 Museum Street, London WC1A 1LU, UK

George Allen & Unwin (Publishers) Ltd,
Park Lane, Hemel Hempstead, Herts HP2 4TE, UK

Allen & Unwin Inc.,
9 Winchester Terrace, Winchester, Mass 01890, USA

George Allen & Unwin Australia Pty Ltd,
8 Napier Street, North Sydney, NSW 2060, Australia

First published in 1983

British Library Cataloguing in Publication Data

Coddington, Alan
    Keynesian economics.
1. Keynes, John Maynard
2. Keynesian economics
I. Title
330.15′6   HB99.7
ISBN 0-04-330334-X

Library of Congress Cataloging in Publication Data

Coddington, Alan
    Keynesian economics.
Bibliography: p.
Includes index.
1. Keynesian economics.   I. Title.
HB99.7.C6 1983   330.15′6   82-20559
ISBN 0-04-330334-X

Set in 10 on 11 point Times
and printed in Great Britain by
Richard Clay (The Chaucer Press) Ltd, Bungay, Suffolk

Contents

Publisher's Note

Alan Coddington had completed and delivered an immaculate final draft of the book, and had only to add a few remaining thoughts and references before his tragic death on June 8th, 1982.
The Publishers wish to thank Mr. Chris Johns and Dr. Colette Bowe for their kind help in ensuring that the text stands as the author had written it and as he would have wished to see it in print.

Preface

In 1971, I was assigned, along with a colleague, to teach a second year undergraduate course in Economic Principles within the University of London B.Sc.(Econ.). Although I thought of myself at that time as a specialist in microeconomic theory, it was nevertheless decided that I should teach the macroeconomic part of 'Principles'. I had taken a macroeconomic theory course in the academic year 1964–5, as one of the core courses in the York D.Phil. programme, a course that had relied very heavily on M. J. Bailey, *National Income and the Price Level*. Almost the only use I had made of this training was in leading, over a period of years, a succession of discussion groups at what was then the Centre for Administrative Studies (later to be transformed into the Civil Service College) for what were then called Assistant Principals. Given the intellectual calibre of the people involved and the fact that they had already, by the time they came on these courses, spent some couple of years in a government department, this was, for me, a rewarding educational experience. Indeed, I am confident that the insights that this afforded me into the working of the government machine and into the modes of thought of the officials within it, were of much greater interest to me than the insights into macroeconomic theory that were supposed to be flowing in the opposite direction were to their recipients. Apart from that, I also had a dim awareness that, at the level of government policy in this country, all was not well with the body of macroeconomic ideas, some fragment of which I had grasped as a graduate student in York.

My first response to the lecturing assignment was to make an excursion, armed with a cheque book, to the Economists Bookshop. One of the books I bought on that occasion looked quite interesting despite its convoluted title and despite the fact that I had never heard of the author. It was called *On Keynesian Economics and the Economics of Keynes* and it bore little resemblance to the kind of thing I remembered from Martin

Bailey. Instead of working out expenditure multipliers under a variety of different assumptions, the author was trying to explain how and why there could be any multiplier process to give rise to the effects represented by these calculations. Quite apart from the substance of the book, there was a question of manner: the impression given was of a far greater sense of intellectual engagement than I had found in the macroeconomics texts of my graduate student days. (After a long period of digestion, it has become possible to take a far more jaundiced view of this particular work, especially looking at it in the light of the developments stemming from it; but this should not be allowed to detract from its undoubted revitalising effects while it was in the process of being assimilated.) In the course of this reading I also recalled that I had, whilst completing my D.Phil. thesis, attended a seminar given in York by Robert Clower: I recalled, too, being impressed not only by the polished and forceful presentation of this seminar, but also by the sense that Clower was exposing fundamental issues that had previously been brushed aside. (He was talking about the theory of the consumption function and what later became known as the dual-decision hypothesis.) In fact, I left the seminar with far more of a sense of the intellectual engagement of the speaker than of comprehension of the issue that had been addressed.

I began to give lectures on macroeconomic theory and to take what I hoped was a more systematic interest in the major issues of policy that fall within the scope of the subject. The result was my papers on 'Economists and policy' (1973) and 'Re-thinking economic policy' (1974b), which together constituted a kind of stock-taking exercise, or a general clearing of the ground in that area where macroeconomic theory and policy meet one another. In the meantime, I gave seminars on Leijonhufvud. In particular, I gave one called 'Leijonhufvud on Keynes' to the LSE Money Workshop in January 1974, at which Charles Goodhart introduced the concept of 'rational expectations', a term I had not previously met. This seminar developed into a piece for the US magazine *Challenge* in November/December 1974: 'What *did* Keynes really mean?' in which I prepared a popularised version of what I then took to be the essence of Leijonhufvud's arguments.

In order to trace another strand in these developments, I have to go back to 1972 when G. L. S. Shackle's *Epistemics and*

Economics was published. I already knew Shackle through his having been the external examiner on my D.Phil. thesis. Shackle sent me a copy of his *Epistemics* book in December of 1972, just in time for me to take it with me to Stockholm, where I was to be for two weeks, principally to act as external examiner along with Oskar Morgenstern on a Ph.D. submitted at the Stockholm School of Economics. The fact that every piece of reading matter at the flat in which I was staying was in Swedish meant that I was able to give a thorough reading to a rather long book.

I was then approached by Imre Lakatos who was planning to devote an issue of the *British Journal for the Philosophy of Science* to philosophical issues within economics. He suggested that, as a contribution to this issue, I should write a review article on Shackle's new book. (Sadly, Lakatos did not live to see this issue materialise, and the remnants of his plans had to be sorted out by Spiro Latsis and John Worrel.) I worked on this review article throughout the summer of 1973 and produced a draft which I circulated for comments later in the year; because of Lakatos's death, however, this did not appear in the *BJPS* until 1975. The closing section of this review article dealt with Shackle's interpretation of Keynes's *General Theory*. Although I have come to take a far more critical attitude than was evident in this review article to Shackle's interpretation of Keynes's work, the experience of getting to grips with Shackle's ideas has nevertheless left its traces: these will become apparent in the chapters that follow, especially 'Deficient Foresight' and 'The Search for First Principles'.

In the academic year 1974–75, I was fortunate enough to be appointed to a Hallsworth Fellowship in Political Economy at the University of Manchester. The chairs in economics were at that time occupied by David Laidler, Michael Parkin and Dennis Coppock; Jack Johnston was still there as Professor of Econometrics; and Alvin Marty was there for a year on a Simon Fellowship. So there was plenty going on. David Laidler and Michael Parkin were running a very active research project, with SSRC finance, on inflation; this involved regular workshops and a great deal of informal, but no less intense, discussions, over coffee, lunch, tea and beyond. As the duties of the Hallsworth Fellow did not include any teaching, this milieu provided me with an excellent opportunity to develop ideas I had been concerned with, and to follow my interests over a much wider range of reading (and talking) than would be possible in the interstices of normal teaching duties and other responsibilities. What the positive obligations of the Hallsworth Fellow were, I was never very sure; no one ever told me. In the event, I took them to include appearing regularly in the common room of the Dover Street building at coffee times, and trying to make myself conversationally agreeable to the various people who came and went, in various degrees of preoccupation and harassment, between their lectures, tutorials and so on. I may say that I settled into this routine very quickly, with the distinct feeling that I was far better equipped for this kind of job than for the more usual kind of academic appointment. Indeed, so conscientiously did I pursue my Dover Street common room responsibilities that sometimes a conversation that had been interrupted when someone had had to leave to teach would be resumed when the person involved came back an hour later, neatly coinciding with the departure of those with whom I had been conversing in the meantime. Despite the fact that it must have been, at least intermittently, somewhat galling for these hard-pressed people to keep encountering me in a perpetually expansive mood, they were, without exception, unfailingly courteous.

It was in Manchester that the outline of this book took shape, although it didn't become clearly visible until 1981. I was asked to give a seminar to the MA students and I said that I would like to talk about Keynesianism. When I came to write the notes for this seminar it struck me that the term 'Keynesianism' is such a portmanteau category that one must, for analytical purposes, make some divisions within it. So I gave the seminar on the basis of the 'three varieties' theme that now permeates this book. Michael Kennedy took an interest in this and was very helpful; indeed he was even more helpful, later, when I had returned to London and he sent me painstaking comments on my drafts of the paper that came out of this theme. The fact that Michael had a thorough knowledge of the literature of applied (to the UK) macroeconomics was also a tremendous help. The other person whose help at this stage I must acknowledge is Thanos Skouras. It was in correspondence with him that my draft was transformed in 1976 into a Thames

Paper in Political Economy with the title *Varieties of Keynesianism*.

It had by this time become apparent to me that, within the literature of Keynesian Economics, there was a school of thought according to which the mainstream of Keynesian ideas had, from the start, been diverted in a retrograde direction. This diversion was supposed to have been instigated by Sir John Hicks, who, as a result, had become symbolic of a wide field of endeavour which his own work was seen as epitomising. In order to achieve this status, what Hicks was supposed to have done was to have taken the pristine work of Keynes's *General Theory* and, via a kind of Walrasian sleight of hand, transformed the profound and intellectually subversive message into something innocuous, insipid and even lifeless. He was supposed to have done this, moreover, on two distinct levels: on a level addressed to his peers (in *Value and Capital*); and on a level that later made contact with undergraduate instruction (in his 'Mr. Keynes and the "Classics" ' with the aid of his IS/LL (later to become IS/LM) construction).

As soon as I began to read Hicks, during my Manchester year, I discovered that I could not believe this piece of demonology. This feeling came not only from reading *Value and Capital*; it was reinforced by the *Critical Essays in Monetary Theory*. So it became clear that, if I were to chart the 'Varieties of Keynesianism', I ought to sort out his – obviously major – role in the story. This gave me an enormous amount of trouble; indeed it was only by leaving Hicks out for separate treatment that I managed to get 'The search for first principles' completed. (This appeared in the *Journal of Economic Literature* in 1976.)

Mark Perlman, the then editor of the *JEL*, knew something of the difficulties I had had, trying to fit Hicks into the story of Keynesianism, and suggested that I should write another piece for the *JEL* dealing just with Hicks's role. This struck me as a very good opportunity to attempt to do what I had for some time felt that I wanted to do, namely, set the record straight on Hicks's having been seized on as a convenient scapegoat for the perceived shortcomings of the textbook manifestation of Keynesian ideas, and, in particular, the failure of this textbook material to live up to the quite extravagant expectations of some of Keynes's closest associates and most ardent followers. Unfortunately, when I came to write down the results of my reflections, they just got longer and longer, and I had to confess to Mark Perlman that my paper had turned into a book. With a great display of diplomatic skill, however, he intimated that the circulation of the *JEL* was far in excess of the likely sales of a possible monograph on a topic which – in book form – would inevitably appear very specialised. I took his point. The result, after a savage cuts exercise, was the piece that came out in the *JEL* in 1979. (I should mention that, in the course of this work, I did not have any contact with Hicks himself; I thought it was appropriate to piece together the story from the published record rather than there being any suggestion that I was acting as a mouthpiece, to whatever extent, for Hicks's own version of the story. Accordingly, although Hicks (via Mark Perlman) knew that I was engaged in this enterprise, he did not see anything of it until the final version was sent to him prior to publication, so that he could contribute a rejoinder to the same issue. I had already corresponded with Hicks on other issues, but not at all in connection with this piece.)

It was also at Mark Perlman's suggestion that I wrote a review article (appearing in the *JEL* in 1978) on Malinvaud's book, appearing in 1977, *The Theory of Unemployment Reconsidered*. This article caused me a good deal of mental anguish, and it was my intention, given its strong thematic links with the present work, somehow to incorporate it in this book. In the end, however, I conceded defeat: its origins as a book review, even if a lengthy one, remained transparently obvious.

In 1977 there were further pressures on me that influenced the way this work turned out: I was assigned to teach an M.Sc. course in Macroeconomic Theory and Policy, a course consisting of some twenty lectures (on theory) and a seminar programme (on applied, policy-oriented questions) run in parallel. In the course of assembling a course outline, seminar topics and reading lists, it was necessary to sort out my ideas about the subject as a whole and, in particular, given the 'theory and policy' set-up, to decide which pieces of theory, on the grounds of their indispensability or close relevance for policy issues, should be included. (Although I had given lectures on 'The reappraisal of Keynesian Economics' as part of the Economic Theory paper on the M.Sc.(Econ.) as previously constituted, I now decided to drop this topic on the grounds of its remoteness from questions of policy-making; some of the work of Clower and Leijonhufvud, however, lingered on in the discussion of the adjustment processes that were supposed to take place within the income/expenditure model, and in the discussion of the aggregative structure of macro-models.) The seminar programme, dealing as it did with the policy problems of the UK economy, led, in an indirect kind of way, to my attempts to distill all this into a reasonably accessible treatment. The result was two talks on BBC Radio 3: 'Hanging on in difficult times' (in 1980) and 'The Economy-sized Budget' (in 1981). My indebtedness to the producer of these talks, Richard Ellis, is considerable: in patiently insisting that my arguments be put in plain and, where possible, vivid terms, he induced me to think more concretely about these things than my training and usual responsibilities would have led me to do. The chapter on 'Demand Deficiency', in this volume, is an exposition of the central themes of the two radio talks, translated back into an idiom more in keeping with the rest of the volume. It is also a manifestation of a long-standing uneasiness I had felt about the concept of 'involuntary unemployment': the tension between its apparent reality as a common-sense idea, and its evident elusiveness as an analytical construct within a wider theoretical scheme.

The chapter on 'Deficient Foresight' arose out of a suggestion made by Jack Wiseman. In 1981, Jack was president of Section F of the British Association, and chose for the topic for the September meeting in York (and for his Presidential Address) 'Beyond Positivism'. His suggestion was that I should tackle some theme connected with subjectivism in economics; we agreed that I should look at the subjectivist stand of thought within Keynesian economics. Although in the event I didn't manage to attend the BA meeting, Jack's suggestion resulted, with some encouragement from Bob Clower along the way, in a further chapter, and one that linked up quite well with the concerns of 'The Search for First Principles', tidying up some of the loose ends from that chapter.

The last chapter to be written was the one on 'The Keynesian Dichotomy'. It occurred to me at a very late stage (and to the consternation of my long-suffering editor at Allen and Unwin, Nicholas Brealey) that this chapter would provide a wider and, I think, more coherent framework than appears elsewhere in the book, within which the whole discussion may be located.

As has already been indicated, two of the chapters in this volume originally appeared in the *Journal of Economic Literature*, and one in the *American Economic Review*. I must therefore express my gratitude to the American Economic Association for granting its permission to use this copyright material.

In addition to those individuals who have already been mentioned as having helped in one way or another, I must also acknowledge my indebtedness to the following people: Jim Ball, Mark Blaug, John Brothwell, Bob Coats, Bernard Corry, Rodney Cross, David Currie, Paul Davidson, Geoffrey Harcourt, Richard Jackman, Chris Johns, the late Harry Johnson, Ludwig Lachman, Brian Loasby, Allan Meltzer, Don Patinkin, Alan Peacock, Joan Robinson, Ekkehart Schlicht, John Williamson and Martin Wright. It must also be said that the astringent intellectual influence of Colette Bowe has pervaded the whole endeavour at every stage of its development.

It remains only to absolve all these people from any responsibility for the inadequacies of this work: these must be counted, even where they lack originality, as my own contribution.

1

Introduction

1. The Keynesian connection

This book is about the efforts of economists to assimilate, develop and refine Keynesian ideas about how an economy may be managed so as to counteract a particular kind of malfunctioning to which it would otherwise be prone. It is especially about their efforts to characterise the precise mode of malfunctioning to which Keynesian policies provide a remedy. As such, it is an exercise in the (recent) history of ideas: but it is concerned primarily with the internal development of those ideas, rather than their influence by, or on, events.

I am not at all concerned with questions of authenticity: neither with what Keynes actually said, nor with what he really meant when he said it, nor even what, according to various guardians of the purity of his thought, he was really trying to say and is only now succeeding in saying through them. (Wide-ranging though Keynes's talents were, I do not believe they extended to posthumous ventriloquism.) This book is a work neither of exegesis nor of hagiography. It is concerned with a cluster of ideas which happen to have become identified with Keynes's name, even if he might have been inclined to disown them had he still been around to do so. I would not bother to make these merely negative points except that a great deal of work in this area has consisted of an – as it appears to me – pointless attempt to excavate and uphold a profound but elusive 'Economics of Keynes' (himself) in contrast with a shallow and vulgar 'Keynesian Economics' (of the textbooks and the public domain).

At the most fundamental level, what distinguishes Keynesian policies is that they take a utilitarian view of the public finances.

1

Following this line of thought, Keynesian economics would be characterised by its capacity to provide a rationale for taking such a view: Keynesian theories and models of economic functioning would, accordingly, be those in which there is some scope for adopting a utilitarian perspective on public finance. Such a utilitarian perspective would be one in which the state of those public finances is not judged to be good or bad in accordance with an 'internal' criterion applying only to the finances themselves, but rather to a criterion involving the consequences for the whole economy of the public finances being arranged or managed in any particular way. It is therefore an application of the utilitarian principle that acts should not be judged good or bad 'in themselves' (according as they fall within particular categories of acts deemed to be good or bad), but only in so far as they promote consequences that are good or bad. There is, however, a problem as to whether these calculations of consequences should apply to individual actions ('act-utilitarianism') or to rules for action ('rule-utilitarianism'), a problem which, in the sphere of economics, has re-surfaced as the debate over 'rules versus discretion' in policy-making. Of course, even if acts, or rules for action, or the state of the public finances, cannot, within a utilitarian perspective, be judged good or bad 'in themselves', the consequences of these various things must be so judged if we are to come to any conclusions. It should be apparent, though, that the 'consequentialist' aspect of utilitarianism, although a necessary part of the philosophy, is separate from the question of the criterion on which consequences are judged. This can be left elastic or even open-ended; the utilitarianism of the nineteenth century was generally hedonistic in this respect, but its descendants in the twentieth century have been disposed to skirt round this issue. It could be argued, for example, that the concept of 'utility' in modern economics is neither hedonistic nor non-hedonistic; it is simply a name for whatever it is people think they want, whatever that may be. (These themes concerning the legacy of utilitarianism to modern economics are elaborated in Coddington, 1976b.) Since it is, I would argue, the *consequentialist* element of the Keynesian perspective on public finance that gives it its distinctive flavour and its characteristic dispositions of thought and action, these complications need not detain us here.

A utilitarian perspective on the public finances may be

contrasted with the idea that there may be precepts of 'sound finance' or financial 'propriety', 'rectitude', 'responsibility' and so on. This is the view that there is a direct parallel between the soundness of the finances of an individual household and the soundness of the finances of government that the difference is merely one of the scale on which funds are raised and disposed of. It is a view that has a strong common-sense appeal, which is why one of the most effective ways of propounding, at the popular level, anti-Keynesian ideas on public finance is to appeal to this analogy by speaking as if the government's financial obligations were simply a matter of housekeeping writ large.

Given its utilitarian perspective, Keynesian thought is faced with two possibilities: either it must reject the parallel between households and governments (so that what would constitute 'responsible' financial conduct for a household cannot be simply scaled up to apply to governments); or it could retain the parallel, but allow it to work in the other direction; that is, from governments to households. This would make individual financial responsibility dependent on economy-wide considerations; it would, for example, make it 'financially irresponsible' for individuals to save in a recession.

In order for a utilitarian perspective to have any implications for the conduct of the public finances it is evident that one must have at one's disposal some systematic, reliable connection between, on the one hand, the way these finances are managed and, on the other hand, the level of activity in the whole economy. Accordingly, to be in a position to carry out Keynesian policies, one needs to establish not just that the management of the public finances will have an effect on the level of economic activity; one needs to establish, or have grounds for believing, that this connection is a reliable one in the sense that it will persist in the face of the general turbulence associated with the functioning of the economy, and, in particular, that it will persist in the face of policy changes aimed at affecting the level of activity. This is an issue that I should like to label the 'leverage problem'; it concerns not so much the existence of a lever as its strength and rigidity. Thus, levers may be ineffective as means of moving a load either because they are too fragile relative to the weight of the load, and so are prone to break when used, or when used at all vigorously; or because they lack rigidity and so, instead of moving the load, change their own shape. What has come to be called the 'Lucas critique' (of macroeconomic policy evaluation via econometric simulations) may be expressed rather simply and graphically in these terms as being the claim that the macroeconomic policy lever is either hopelessly wobbly or brittle, to a degree that makes the consequences of pulling it quite unpredictable, other than the prediction that it will increase the general amount of confusion that there is as to what is happening (Lucas, 1976). Another, closely related, idea is one that has come to be known as 'Goodhart's Law': the claim that relationships between monetary aggregates and other aggregates persist precisely to the extent that such relationships are not exploited as a means to controlling these other aggregates. This is evidently a thoroughly jaundiced view. It gives to the monetary lever a kind of tantalising existence that is the exact opposite of the light in the refrigerator: the light comes on only when you need it, but the monetary lever is there only when you don't need it.

In summary, then, it can be said that the advocacy of a Keynesian approach to the public finances depends not just on there being grounds for the belief in the connection to which I have been referring in terms of 'leverage', but rather on there being grounds for a belief in the *reliability* of that connection. There is then a question of 'How reliable?'; a question which the lever analogy may help us to see cannot be answered in a contextual vacuum. How reliable the connection must be depends on how ambitious the proposed policies are: a brittle lever may withstand gentle pressure but not wild lunges or sudden jerks.

Against this background, Keynesian economics may be seen as the search for this connection, together with the task of providing grounds for the belief in its reliability. In particular, Keynesian economic theory may be seen as the task of analytically uncovering and isolating such a connection, together with the associated task of providing it with a rationale: with arguments in support of a belief in the reliability of the connection. This search for the 'Keynesian connection', and for its rationale, has posed such deep analytical problems that, as well as generating a substantial body of theory, they merge over into matters of analytical method and, beyond that, into epistemology. It is this search for the Keynesian connection that is the subject matter of this book; specifically, this book is concerned with what I believe to be the most important ideas and arguments that have appeared in the course of this search.

2. Outline of the argument

If the level of activity in the economy is responsive to the total expenditure on domestically-produced output, and if the government, via its management of the public finances, may make net additions to (or net subtractions from) this total of expenditure, then there exists a channel through which the Keynesian connection may operate. This argument evidently contains two premises: one is the responsiveness of domestically-produced output to the level of expenditure; the other is the ability of the government systematically to influence the level of expenditure. The connection may, accordingly, fail for two reasons: either the unresponsiveness of domestic activity to changes in total expenditure (an expenditure increase may be met by price rises or inventory decumulation rather than an increase in activity); or the uncontrollability of total expenditure via the influence of the management of the public finances (changes in the government's net contribution to total expenditure may be offset by changes in other components of expenditure, changes which, in turn, may be either haphazard or may be induced by the changes in the public finances themselves: in the latter case, for example, it may happen that the government's contribution to total expenditure is offset, either partially or totally, by a resulting reduction ('crowding out') of expenditures that would otherwise have occurred).

Chapter 2, 'The Keynesian Dichotomy', deals with the basis for one link in the Keynesian connection: the link between total expenditure and the level of domestic activity. It presents this link, however, as part of a wider analytical procedure, a procedure in which the general level of prices makes an appearance within the other side of the dichotomy. The other side of the dichotomy is one in which, subject to some qualifications, the general level of prices is related to the general level of costs. The 'Keynesian dichotomy' is presented, in Chapter 2, as an alternative analytical procedure to that embodied in the so-called 'classical dichotomy' in accordance with which the 'real' and 'monetary' aspects of the economy may, subject to some qualifications, be analysed separately from one another.

Once one begins to think about macroeconomic policy in the context of the Keynesian dichotomy, two corollaries follow immediately. The first is that the level of total expenditure that happens to obtain at any given time may not correspond to a desirable level of activity – as manifest by the level of output relative to trend or by the level of registered unemployment, for example – for the economy as a whole. The second corollary is that the level (or rate of change over time) of costs may not correspond to a desirable level (or rate of change over time) of the index of prices.

The former corollary leads directly to the concept of 'demand deficiency', and the associated need for a rationale for using this concept as a diagnostic tool. This concept and the problems of providing such a rationale are discussed at some length in Chapter 3. This chapter also addresses, although in a sketchier way, the corresponding problems in the case of the second corollary of the Keynesian dichotomy. These problems I have brought together into a form I shall refer to as 'the doctrine of instrument deficiency'. This discussion should make it clear why it is no mere accident or coincidence that those who advocate a Keynesian approach to the public finances should also favour prices and incomes policy (in one or other of its many varieties) as a means of countering inflation.

In Chapter 4, we begin to dig deeper. Behind the concept of 'demand deficiency' there must lie some reasons, or even some mechanisms, to account for the variability of expenditure aggregates. One possibility, the elaboration of which has been a perennial theme with Keynesian theory, is that the variability of certain expenditure aggregates – in particular, private sector investment expenditure – may be attributed to what, for the moment, we shall have to be content to call limitations on the decision-making capacities of individual agents. This theme has been used as the vehicle for analysis much of which, in my view, is muddled and obscurantist. In Chapter 4, I try to sort out these issues. In particular, I ask whether and how the alleged limitations on the decision-making capacities of individual agents could contribute either to the government's need or to its ability to exploit the Keynesian connection. The issue, as we shall see, turns not on whether there are deficiencies of foresight, but rather on whether there are *differences* in such deficiency as between expenditure categories and as between sectors of the economy; there is a more fundamental issue, too, of whether and, if so, how, deficiencies of foresight lead to greater variability of expenditure aggregates than would otherwise be the case. Here we discover a deficiency in a standard theme in Keynesian theorising: a missing step in the argument.

After Chapter 4, there is a change of gear. Having examined Keynesian ideas in a way that was organised around analytical issues, we turn, in Chapters 5 and 6, to organise them around the work of particular individuals and schools of thought. The reader will be well aware that the term 'Keynesian', although apparently indispensable, is so elastic as to be incapable of serving as a suitable category for use in discussion the (recent) history of economic analysis. Quite apart from schools that spend a good deal of their intellectual efforts disowning one another and trying, in each case, to demonstrate their own Keynesian pedigree, one is also faced with the problem that Keynesianism, like most doctrines, comes in weaker and stronger versions, the weaker of which may be defended with great reasonableness, but the stronger of which is actually required as a basis for practical decision-making (when advising, say, the Chancellor of a government in office).

In order to allow some degree of discrimination within this uproar, I have divided Keynesianism into three schools, recognising that the compartments are not wholly water-tight, and that there may be some anomalous cases who cannot be fitted readily into one or other school. (Indeed I know that this is so, as I have received letters from the anomalous cases themselves, explaining the difficulties they had in slotting themselves into my scheme.)

With these caveats in mind, it can be said that Chapter 6 provides a perspective on the development of Keynesian economic theory over the past twenty years or so. The idea is to give a wide-angle view of the whole field, leaving to one side the various points of analytical detail that have been dealt with in Chapters 2 to 4. Chapter 6, however, as those readers who have not skipped the Preface will know, leaves to one side the part played by Hicks in the unfolding of the Keynesian drama. This part, in my view, is not only a central one, it is also sufficiently contentious to merit separate and detailed treatment. This is provided in Chapter 5.

As each chapter contains its own section of concluding remarks, the concluding chapter to the book is correspondingly brief.

2

The Keynesian Dichotomy

1. Introduction

From the standpoint of pure theory, the most fundamental issue raised by Keynes in the *General Theory* lay in his attack on the traditional separation of monetary and value theory, the 'classical dichotomy' as (following Don Patinkin) it has come to be called, according to which relative prices are determined by the 'real' forces of demand and supply and the absolute price level is determined by the quantity of money and its velocity of circulation. (The reference is to Patinkin, 1949.)

Thus Johnson (1965, p. 2) expresses, with the benefit of three decades of hindsight, what he understands to have been the essence of Keynes's engagement with 'pure theory'. In doing so, Johnson perpetuates the common practice of speaking of this engagement in the language of combat, as Keynes's *attack* on some 'traditional' or 'orthodox' teaching (a practice that was clearly embodied in a generation of textbooks in which this engagement appeared as a contest: 'Keynes *versus* the "classics"'.) Although Johnson is no doubt correct in identifying what was – from the standpoint of pure theory – most fundamental in this engagement, he was, as I hope will become apparent in due course, begging important questions of pure theory by his acceptance of Keynes's engagement at its face value, as a conflict between mutually exclusive theoretical alternatives.

To be more specific about this issue of the classical dichotomy, Chapter 17 of Keynes's *General Theory* may be read as a catalogue of difficulties that stand in the way of keeping separate and distinct the 'real' and the 'monetary' aspects of economic phenomena; in combative language, this becomes transmogrified into an 'attack on the classical dichotomy'. This particular theme has greatly exercised some of Keynes's followers and the commentators on his work: it was taken up and forcefully elaborated by Townshend (1937), and has been extensively and eloquently aired by Shackle (1967, 1974). It has, moreover, been given canonical status by those followers of Keynes whom I shall later label 'fundamentalist'.

In cataloguing the difficulties that stand in the way of the 'classical dichotomy' providing a clean and straightforward analytical decomposition, however, one does not thereby establish that this particular approach should be rejected; nor are matters changed if the emphasis on these difficulties is elevated to a matter of principle. By dwelling on these difficulties, one establishes, if anything, only that dichotomising should be performed with care. For the function of the 'classical dichotomy' is to make theorising more manageable; to make theorising more manageable requires drastic simplification; for critics to point out that these simplifications are, indeed, drastic, is therefore not, in itself, a particularly cogent or damaging response. Given that theorising will be conducted somehow, the only potentially effective way of criticising one manner of providing drastic simplification is to provide an alternative method that can be shown to be superior in some important respect. As Keynesian economics constitutes not only, negatively, a critique of a system of theory that has been labelled 'classical', but also, constructively, an alternative system of theory, we are entitled to expect that it must contain something that is, analytically, the functional equivalent of the 'classical dichotomy': a drastic simplification that makes theorising manageable to the extent that the simplification is accepted. In the following discussion, I shall, first, isolate what I take to be the drastic simplification that is at the heart of the Keynesian system; second, I shall attempt to explain how this 'Keynesian dichotomy' operates, and how its adoption might be justified; and, third, I shall address the question of how these two dichotomies stand in relation to one another.

2. The Keynesian dichotomy

What I am going to maintain is that there is a characteristically Keynesian analytical procedure which may be thought of as a 'dichotomy' in much the same way as characteristically 'classical' analytical procedures may be encapsulated in the principle of the classical dichotomy. Of course, just as the classical dichotomy requires various qualifications to allow departures from its strict operation, so we may reasonably expect the Keynesian dichotomy to be hedged with various caveats. The task to which I now turn is that of expounding the manner of operation of the Keynesian dichotomy; this task I envisage as being in the nature of a discussion of case law: a problem of the distillation of principles from an existing and evolving body of practice.

The Keynesian dichotomy, in its basic, unqualified form, may be stated as the principle that output is determined by aggregate demand, and that prices are determined by costs.
Thus we read, for example:

Demand takes on its Keynesian role as effective demand as the determinant of output, only to the extent that it is separated from the movement of prices. (Shapiro, 1977, p. 550)

Further:

The other half of the Keynesian revolution was to recognise that, in an industrial economy, the level of prices is governed primarily by the level of money-wage rates. (Robinson, 1973, p. 6)

Again:

In other words in the short term (which here means at least two years) the pressure of demand makes no difference to the price level. (Godley, 1976, p. 308)

And again:

Prices in the U.K., apparently, are determined by only one blade of Marshall's scissors. (Blinder, 1978, p. 74)

Blinder is referring to the Featherston and Godley price equation, and, in particular, to the absence of a demand pressure term in that equation (in contrast to the corresponding price equations in US models). (See also Blinder, 1978, pp. 75, 82.)

It may readily be seen that the basic separation imposed by the principle of the Keynesian dichotomy is into two subsystems: one in which the level of output is determined; and another in which the price level is determined. I shall refer to the first part of the dichotomy, involving the determination of output by aggregate demand, as the hydraulic principle (The reasons for this designation, if they are not apparent, will be explained in Chapter 6.) The second part of the dichotomy, involving the determination of prices by costs, I shall refer to, in a more conventional way, as the mark-up principle. It should be evident that the hydraulic principle is to be found embodied in the simple income/expenditure models of elementary textbooks (models which lack any treatment of a financial sector) and the associated simple multiplier results; it should also be evident that the mark-up principle is to be found embodied in 'cost-push' (and, in particular, 'wage-push') theories of inflation.

In order to see what qualifications need to be made to the principle of the Keynesian dichotomy, we may enquire, first, under what conditions it would work strictly; we may then seek the qualifications that correspond to the departures from these 'ideal' conditions. It is not hard to see, accordingly, that the hydraulic principle requires, for its strict applicability, the condition that aggregate supply is perfectly elastic at the prevailing price level; that is to say, that the aggregate supply curve is horizontal. Similarly, it is a straightforward matter to see that the mark-up principle requires, for its strict applicability, the condition that aggregate demand is perfectly inelastic with respect to price-level changes; that is to say, that the aggregate demand curve is vertical. In such conditions, a change in costs shifts the aggregate supply curve, but the consequences of this are confined to price-level effects.

All this, however, is unsatisfactory in that it makes no mention of money or finance. In order to bring these things into the picture, even in the most rudimentary way, we may adopt the IS/LM framework of analysis. This will then allow us to examine the conditions for the strict operation of the first part of the Keynesian dichotomy: the hydraulic principle. The IS/

LM framework, however, is one in which the price level appears exogenously (in the LM curve); it cannot, accordingly, provide a context in which the conditions for the strict operation of the mark-up principle may be explored. (Although, of course, the exogeneity of the price level in this framework makes it entirely compatible with a mark-up principle: it is, in itself, perfectly receptive, if the price level is to be made endogenous to the model, to the addition of a mark-up principle to determine this variable.) In fact, the exploration of this second part of the Keynesian dichotomy has manifest itself not in the context of the IS/LM framework (and the various relationships from which it is composed) but, rather, in the context of price equations and wage equations. (Such equations typically operate in the realm of first differences, so that what they are concerned with are the rates of price and wage inflation.) The empirical correctness of the mark-up principle hinges on whether some index of demand pressure is a statistically significant variable in price equations. If, however, it is already taken for granted, as part of the specification of wage/price interactions, that the price level is related to the wage level by a mark-up rule, the empirical issue is transposed to the domain of wage equations: if the wage level is found to be impervious to demand-pressure effects, then the specification entails that the price level is also free from them.

The condition for the strict operation of the hydraulic principle is, within the context of the IS/LM framework, that the demand for money must be perfectly interest-elastic; that is to say, the LM curve must be horizontal. In other words, the hydraulic principle operates to the extent that the interest rate mechanism is prevented from doing so; this is a circumstance that may arise either through the actions of the monetary authorities (in 'pegging' the interest rate) or through the actions of traders on financial markets (in acting on the general belief that the interest rate must be going to rise to an extent that would entail capital losses in excess of interest gains for bond-holders.) We may accordingly see the hydraulic principle as a special case of a more general principle of economic functioning. The more general principle is that a change in aggregate expenditure (a reduction, say) will be met partly by a reduction in output, and partly by a reduction in the interest rate such as to counteract, to some extent, the reduction in output that would otherwise have ensued. If we start from this more general principle, we arrive at the special case relevant to the Keynesian dichotomy if we consider the interest rate mechanism to be – for whatever reason – out of action, so that all the burden of adjustment is thrown onto changes in output.

(In fact, if the price level were allowed to take part, as a potentially equilibrating variable, in the adjustment processes resulting from aggregate expenditure changes, we could see the hydraulic principle as a special case of a still more general principle. It would be the case in which the price level effects were either absent (perhaps because of the time scale with which one was concerned) or were, in ways that we shall encounter presently, either neutralised or prevented by policy actions. It is worth noting, incidentally, that the standard textbook method of distinguishing between different 'time scales' has nothing at all to do with time, but depends instead on which of these three potentially equilibrating variables is excluded from the adjustment process: namely, the price level in the 'short-run', and real output in the 'long-run'.)

We now turn to the issues connected with the operation of the mark-up principle; in particular, to the question of its underlying rationale. By pursuing this question of the principle's rationale, it should be possible, as with the preceding discussion of the hydraulic principle, to gain, first, an understanding of the conditions required for its strict operation, and, thereby, some idea of the wider set of conditions in which it may be expected to provide a reasonable first approximation to the processes it purports to represent.

The mark-up model of pricing is also sometimes referred to as the 'full cost' model, to emphasize, presumably, its divergence from any price-setting principle that depends on a concept of marginal cost. The switching of attention from marginal to average costs, however, is by no means the whole story: the mark-up model also introduces a notion of 'normal' costs, by which is meant what costs *would* be if the economy were operating at some standardised level of capacity utilization, rather than at the level that corresponds to the actual cyclical state that it happens to be in. The essential idea of the mark-up principle is, accordingly, that prices are related to the underlying trend of costs rather than to their cyclically fluctuating manifestation: 'normal' costs are to be understood, therefore, as 'de-cycled' costs.

Prices that are based on such de-cycled costs will evidently not fluctuate as much over the cycle as would prices that were continuously adjusted to cyclical variations in cost conditions. The 'stylised fact' that may be accounted for by a model of this type is the absence of cyclical variation in prices; or, in a qualified form, the absence of as strong a cyclical variation in prices as would be manifest by continuous adjustment of prices to (cyclically varying) costs (see, for example, Neild, 1963, p.2).

The rationale of all this actually hinges on the supposed behaviour of money wages. The 'stylised fact' here is that money wages are impervious to cyclical fluctuations: that there is simply an underlying trend in money wages, which, as far as pricing rules are concerned, must be taken as given. The qualified version of this 'stylised fact' would be that any cyclical variation in money wages is far less than would be implied by the degree of money-wage flexibility (and thereby real-wage flexibility) sufficient to eliminate continuously any excess supply of labour. This behaviour of money wages must then be taken in conjunction with one further stylised fact: namely, that output varies proportionately more than employment over the cycle. Given these assumptions about the cyclical behaviour of money wages, output and employment, it follows that unit labour costs will vary cyclically (in fact, counter-cyclically.) Hence, if prices were continuously adjusted to cyclical conditions, one would expect them to move (counter-) cyclically (unless, of course, there was a cyclical variation of demand just sufficient to offset the cyclical variation in unit costs.) To the extent, therefore, that this cyclical variation is not observed (and the variation in unit labour costs shows up in profits) it follows that prices are set in relation to some concept of de-cycled costs, and, in particular, to some notion of unit labour costs calculated at a standardised ('normal') level of capacity utilization.

What I propose to do next is to pick up the threads of the previous discussion, and to deal with some unfinished business concerning the hydraulic principle. It will be recalled that the condition for the strict operation of this principle is the existence of a 'liquidity trap': a perfectly interest-elastic demand for money, expressing itself as a horizontal LM curve. If this were the whole story, one could reasonably conclude, on purely empirical grounds, that the hydraulic principle is never strictly applicable, and that it provides, at best, a crude first-approximation to the effects of aggregate expenditure changes. The relevant evidence to which appeal could be made would be that in which tests were conducted in which the aim was to detect the existence of a perfectly interest-elastic demand for money at some low rate of interest; the method employed in these investigations was to test the (much weaker) proposition that the interest-elasticity is greater at lower interest rates. These tests, although far from clear-cut in their results, have been such as to make it rather hard to believe in the practical relevance of a 'liquidity trap' (see Laidler, 1977, pp. 130–3).

In fact, the issue of the applicability of the hydraulic principle need not hinge on this particular empirical question. The strict operation of this principle is something which, despite a counteracting interest-rate mechanism, may be rehabilitated with the aid of a supplementary argument about the accommodative role that monetary policy may take in conjunction with fiscal changes. On this line of argument, the hydraulic principle (and with it the 'simple multiplier') becomes, after all, the appropriate way of thinking about the effects of changes in fiscal policy.

The argument is that, within the IS/LM framework, the reason that a fiscal expansion (say) is prevented, by an offsetting interest-rate increase, from having its full hydraulic effect on output is that the fiscal expansion is pushing against a fixed money supply. The authorities may accordingly be seen as pushing with one hand (fiscal expansion), but resisting this push with the other hand (monetary non-accommodation); and if monetary non-accommodation is seen as a deliberate act of policy, the rise in the interest rate must appear as a self-inflicted wound. On such a view, the authorities are simply making life difficult for themselves by getting in each other's way. If the fiscal and monetary authorities were only to co-ordinate their efforts, there is no reason, on this view, why they should not jointly bring about the strict operation of the hydraulic principle. So, from a Radcliffian point of view – if one takes it as being the proper concern of the monetary authorities to stabilize interest rates (that is, to seek to peg them at some 'appropriate' level) – the hydraulic principle emerges quite naturally, not as a principle of spontaneous economic functioning, but as a target at which macroeconomic policies could reasonably be expected to aim. Such, at any rate, is the case within the fix-price world of the standard IS/LM framework.

The argument, however, is easily extended beyond the fix-price context. That is to say, it may be extended to a further process whereby the real effects of fiscal expansion may be undermined: increases in the price level that potentially counteract these real effects may be offset, on the same argument as we have just encountered, by an extra dose of monetary accommodation, in addition to that already required to peg the rate of interest. Of course, to maintain such an accommodative policy, the monetary authorities must commit themselves to the possibility of a race against inflation: they must, in addition to the requirements of pegging the interest rate, continue to arrange for monetary expansion to match the existing rate of inflation, even if this accelerates, and even if it accelerates as a consequence of the policies that are being pursued. The fact that the authorities may find themselves in a race against the consequences of their own actions is quite without prejudice to the issue of whether these inflationary consequences are attributable to the monetary policies alone, or to some wider package of policies.

Even the most resolute expansionist, however, can hardly relish the prospect of chasing after the inflation rate, no matter how rapid it may be. Accordingly, it has become a commonplace for those who advocate Keynesian fiscal and monetary policies to advocate also that policies be devised and implemented which provide the price level with some form of anchorage ('prices and incomes policy'). The argument behind this is that if engineered expansions tend to dissipate themselves in price level increases, it is necessary to hold down the price level at the same time as pursuing aggregate demand policies; in this way, the aggregate demand policies should – provided the price level *is* held down – have their effect on real output. Along these lines of argument the hydraulic principle emerges, yet again, as a potentiality: as something to be aimed at by a suitably enlarged assembly of policies. This is a theme to which we shall return in Chapter 3.

It should now be apparent that the hydraulic principle, no matter what its shortcomings as a representation of spontaneous economic functioning, may always be salvaged as an objective of a sufficiently extended assembly of policies. This conclusions arises, however, not because of anything that is present in the

Keynesian system, but because of what is absent: it arises because the Keynesian system lacks a theory of the allocation of resources. In the absence of an explicit treatment of allocation, resources have to be placed, analytically speaking, into one of two categories: those that are allocated in some way or other ('employed') and those that are not allocated at all ('unemployed'). Implicit in all this is the idea that there is no opportunity cost in bringing into use any of the 'unemployed' resources (up to some evanescent limit of 'full employment'.) The fact that apparent failures of Keynesian theory may always be transformed into apparently constructive proposals for the extension of the scope of policy is entirely a manifestation of this suppression of allocation problems. What this line of argument amounts to, then, is the view that, if there is an opportunity to get something for nothing, the important thing is to avail oneself of that opportunity, on the understanding that the precise manner of obtaining it can presumably always be worked out somehow. The Keynesian system addresses itself to some of the problems of availing oneself of an opportunity which it takes for granted is of such a straightforwardly attractive kind.

3.   Dichotomies as analytical procedures

In the previous section of this chapter, the object has been to isolate the analytical procedures that provide the Keynesian system with its central organising principle: with what, in its unqualified use, provides the drastic simplification that enables such analysis to reach definite conclusions. We have also been concerned with the lines along which a justification might be found for the adoption of such procedures. In the present section, the aim will be to stand back somewhat to consider the analytical function of 'dichotomies' generally, and to try to see, in particular, how the classical and Keynesian ones stand in relation to one another. A further aim in what follows is to prepare the ground for the recurrence of this issue – as a matter of some importance in the work of Hicks – in Chapter 5.

As I have observed in the opening section of this chapter, in order to make analysis manageable one has to simplify, and simplify drastically. I also pointed out, at the same time, that a most effective kind of simplification is one in which, for analytical purposes, a system under investigation may be *decomposed*: that is, thought of as two sub-systems, each functioning with a certain degree of autonomy.

How may we justify the adoption of the procedures embodied in such a dichotomy? Taking a pragmatic view, we may say that a decomposition of the system will be a useful one in so far as it allows analysis to be carried out in stages: that is, in so far as the analysis of interactions *within* each sub-system may be carried out separately from the analysis of interactions *between* the two sub-systems. There are various grounds on which a justification for such a procedure could be offered. The grounds most relevant to the procedures considered in this chapter are ones involving the *time scale* on which the various modes of interaction are believed to operate. Suppose, for example, there are K-phenomena which operate on an appreciably shorter time scale than C-phenomena. In that case we could distinguish between two kinds of dichotomy: a C-dichotomy in which the C-phenomena are treated explicitly, but the K-phenomena appear only as informal qualifications (about 'short-run effects'); and a K-dichotomy in which the K-phenomena are treated explicitly, but the C-phenomena appear only as informal qualifications (about 'long-run effects').

This account of analytical 'dichotomies' makes it plain that both the investigation of interactions within sub-systems and also the investigation of interactions between sub-systems are stages within an overall analytical procedure, or components of a larger analytical whole. The problems arise, however, when we come to enquire how the results of the various stages are to be combined or, at least, how the considerations of the later stages are to be used to provide qualifications of the results arrived at in the earlier stages of the procedure. All this may be made more specific by considering the stages in the procedures corresponding to the classical and the Keynesian dichotomies.

First, in accordance with the classical dichotomy, an analysis would be carried out of the working of the 'real' sub-system (the theory of resource allocation) and of the monetary sub-system. These two together would provide the 'first approximation' of the classical procedure. At the second stage, to complete the procedure, some attention would have to be given to the interactions between the real and monetary sub-systems. The results of this attention would then appear as qualifications to, or complications on, the 'first approximations' already arrived at. It is characteristic, however, of any such dichotomised procedure that the introduction of the second-stage qualifications cannot be made nearly so formal and explicit as can the results that appear as 'first approximations'. Accordingly, this second stage will, unavoidably, appear as a kind of analytical twilight, in which strict and formal analysis provides a fading light for the discernment of shadowy overall outlines by a process which, in the circumstances, has to be largely impressionistic. All of which helps to explain why dichotomies tend to become known by, and held responsible for, the *first* approximations to which they give rise: these are the most definite and the only ostensibly decisive results with which the dichotomies are associated.

Second, consider a procedure based on the Keynesian dichotomy. The first stage of such a procedure would concentrate on analysing interactions between real and monetary phenomena. In order to make this possible, the conceptions of the real and of the monetary phenomena involved have to be schematised to such a degree as would make this analysis manageable. The second stage of the Keynesian procedure, therefore, would be concerned with the qualifications that must be made to the results that appear as 'first approximations': those qualifications concerning the operation of real and of monetary phenomena that had been suppressed in the first stage, but which cannot, in practice, be entirely ignored. As with the classical case, this second-stage discussion will merge over into informality, impressionism and matters of the judgement of the analyst.

The two procedures therefore offer us the following alternatives:

(1) We may first analyse real and monetary phenomena separately and then qualify this 'classical' first approximation by a consideration of the interactions *between* the two phenomena.

(2) We may first analyse interactions between monetary and real phenomena, and then qualify this Keynesian 'first approximation' by a consideration of the neglected interactions *within* each of the spheres of monetary and of real phenomena.

If we were to make comparisons between the two procedures, it should be evident that the appropriate juxtaposition should not involve only the two 'first approximations'; it should involve, if anything, the 'second approximations' consisting of the first-stage results subject to second-stage qualifications. It then follows that there is absolutely no reason why the same conclusions should not be reached by either procedure. Any result that could be arrived at by the classical procedure could be arrived at also by the Keynesian procedure, with the difference that considerations appearing explicitly in the first stage of the classical procedure will appear as qualifications in the second stage of the Keynesian procedure; and *vice versa*. So one might be tempted to conclude that the choice between the two ways of proceeding is merely a matter of convenience. This, however, would not be quite correct. For the considerations that appear *explicitly* (in the first stage of the procedure) differ as between the two approaches: those that appear explicitly in the first stage of one have to be brought in informally in the second stage of the other. As the principal virtue of economic analysis is its capacity to make fully explicit those considerations about which one happens to be most concerned, it cannot be a matter of indifference which procedures to adopt in any particular instance. Although the overall coverage of both procedures is, in principle, the same, they differ in *focus*: what is brought into sharp outline in one, remains hazy and indistinct in the other. (It will be noted that photographers do not engage in doctrinal disputes on such issues as whether close focusing is or is not a better representation of the world than distant focusing; photographers are engaged in a sufficiently down-to-earth activity to be able to see the futility of such a dispute. Unfortunately, the greater remoteness of economic analysis from practical concerns and pursuits has left ample scope for those who happen to be interested in, as it were, foreground objects, to make it an issue of principle that distant focusing is erroneous, misguided and outmoded: something that has been overtaken and superseded by the Close-up Revolution.)

In the preceding discussion, it has been suggested that the way in which the classical and Keynesian dichotomies may be reconciled with one another is by a consideration of the time scale of operation of the phenomena that are in each case focused upon. It should not be supposed, however, that this discussion stands or falls with the feasilibity of this particular mode of reconciliation. D. H. Robertson, for example, conceived of their reconciliation in terms of a consideration of the normality or pathology of operation of the system, rather than the time scale on which particular phenomena unfold; in this way he was led to the view that the classical dichotomy is applicable in cases where the monetary system is operating in such a way as to reveal or interpret the ('underlying') real conditions in the economy, rather than to disguise or distort them (see Robertson, 1966, p. 203). If this account were to be accepted of the domain of applicability of the classical dichotomy (that is to say, of the 'first approximation' that it provides), it would follow that the Keynesian dichotomy (or rather, again, the 'first approximation' that it provides) would emerge as a candidate for application to episodes of monetary disorder and malfunctioning. A consequence of such a mode of reconciliation would be that judgements of the scope of the Keynesian approach would be dependent on broad judgements about the extent to which the type of economy in which we find ourselves is susceptible to such disorder and malfunctioning: a consequence that is entirely consistent with the embattled, protracted and ideologically charged character of the debate in this area.

4. Concluding Remarks

In this chapter, I have presented Keynes's engagement with pure theory as, negatively, a departure from the analytical procedure associated with the classical dichotomy, and, at the same time, as, constructively, the replacement of this dichotomy by an alternative set of procedures corresponding to what I have termed the Keynesian dichotomy. This way of seeing Keynes's involvement with pure theory is in marked contrast with its presentation as having achieved an *integration* of the theories of value and of money (which is evidently what Keynes himself believed that he had done.) For such an 'integration' must surely consist in uniting the theories that were previously separated, not in providing a different mode of separation that cuts across those previously existing theories.

In the light of the preceding discussion (a discussion which will be elaborated in the chapters that follow, especially in

Chapters 5 and 6) it should be apparent that the previously existing (classical) theory of value has not, within the Keynesian approach, been 'integrated' with anything at all; rather, it has been suppressed in the interests of concentrating attention on some aspects of the interaction between monetary and real phenomena. Similarly, and with the same purpose, the classical theory of money has had to be overridden in favour of something both more rudimentary and more in keeping with the particular analytical tasks that Keynes and his followers set themselves (a theme that will recur in Chapter 5). We must conclude, therefore, that what has been widely seen as an 'integration' would be far better described as a 're-focusing'.

3

Demand Deficiency

1. Introduction

Although governments have come to accept that they have responsibilities that require the formulation and execution of a policy towards unemployment, the nature and extent of these responsibilities remain, even after several decades of their being recognised, a highly contentious and politically sensitive matter. The responsibility for alleviating the hardships of the unemployed is the less contentious aspect of the matter. Much more contentious is the question of the government's responsibility for influencing the scale of the problem, there still being a major diagnostic problem in establishing the extent to which unemployment at any time is symptomatic of those disorders for which governments have some form of remedy. Thus, although the question of the nature and extent of government responsibility, in this as in any other sphere, appears to be a nakedly political matter, it is in fact not independent of technical, diagnostic problems. There is accordingly a strong linkage, in the discussion of unemployment policy, between the ideological and the technical spheres of discourse, in that ideological positions presuppose the answer to technical questions, and what are really technical issues appear to have an immediate ideological significance.

The central question addressed by this chapter is whether the concept of 'involuntary unemployment' is capable of performing, or assisting in the performance of, these technical, diagnostic tasks. In raising this issue, one can hardly escape the ideological overtones that any such discussion must have. The aim, however, will be, in addressing the issues that arise when unemployment is seen as a matter for government concern and action, to contribute to the disentangling of the technical from the ideological.

One of the ways in which the subject of economics develops is via a juxtaposition of, and interplay between, on the one hand, common-sense and everyday ideas and, on the other hand, a number of tightly specified frameworks within which the every-day ideas may or may not be accommodated. Sometimes it is possible, by the imposition of some well-specified framework of analysis, to display the inadequacy or even confusion of everyday ideas. Sometimes, however, the influence is in the other direc-tion, and the difficulties of accommodating an everyday, common-sense idea within a formal framework serve to display the inadequacies of the framework, and its need for modification.

One way in which the present discussion may accordingly be seen is as a record of the attempts to adapt the framework of economic theory to allow the accommodation of the phenomenon of 'involuntary unemployment', this latter idea being understood as a brute fact of experience, to demonstrate which it is necessary only to point to the experience of the 1930s, or even the 1980s, (in the UK or USA, say). The supposition here is that the *scale* of the unemployment reveals its *nature*: that *mass* unemployment must be *involuntary*. If involuntary unemploy-ment is accordingly seen as a manifest fact of experience, then the associated analytical task has a clear aim: to develop a framework in which such a thing is at least possible; better still, intelligible; and, best of all, subject to influence by government policy.

In contrast to this way of looking at the issue, there are those who have seen involuntary unemployment as an idea in need of scrutiny, this scrutiny to be effected by finding out whether and how the idea can be accommodated within the appropriate analytical framework. But which is the appropriate one? Is it one that is yet available? This way of proceeding refuses, of course, to see mass unemployment as a phenomenon, the involuntariness of which is manifest to all with eyes to see. Rather, it treats the experience of the 1930s (and, presumably, the 1980s) as historical episodes in need of analysis and interpretation, it being a matter for the accumulated weight of research findings – rather than common-sense intuition – to determine how this mass unemployment is most appropriately interpreted. This approach is therefore not just a matter of disagreement over interpretation: it is a disagreement over research procedures. In particular, it is a disagreement over whether the particular interpretation one places on 'mass unemployment' is something one can begin with, in approaching this field of study, or whether it is something that should be allowed to emerge from one's efforts in that field.

It may therefore be said that there is a quite fundamental issue as to the extent to which, in giving it analytical expression, unemployment should be 'voluntarised'. As we shall see, the alliance of choice theory and a concentration on market-clearing states has voluntarising tendencies of a relentlessness that even the most determined common-sense opposition finds hard to combat. Thus, in the 1930s, those wishing to dispute and combat these voluntarising tendencies had a hard time deciding at what point their common sense could dig in its heels; more especially, they were faced with the problem of finding something to dig their heels *into*. The answer, of course, came along in the shape of Keynes's (1936) *General Theory* which, in the terminology of the present discussion, could be seen as having, as its main thrust, the *de*-voluntarising of the theory of labour supply. In contrast, the upshot of the more recent work on search theory applied to labour markets (for those who allow themselves to be influenced by it) is its *re*-voluntarising. The analytical issues involved have accordingly been played out as a very slow-motion tug-of-war in which no one knows how to recognise when the game is over or whether there can ever be a winning side.

2.   Involuntary unemployment

The understanding of unemployment raises two related questions: a diagnostic question (what kind of unemployment is it?) and a question of responsibility. This question of responsibility, on examination, resolves itself into a further two issues: on the one hand, the issue of the responsibility for alleviating the hardships of unemployment, and, on the other, the issue of the responsibility for reducing its scale. It has been recognised that the attempts by governments to exercise the first of these responsibilities may, through its effects on the incentives to seek employment, interfere with and possibly undermine their attempts to reduce the scale of unemployment. (Just how directly the two responsibilities conflict remains a contentious issue which, as far as the present discussion is concerned, need not detain us any further.)

The concept of involuntary unemployment, as well as having diagnostic uses to which we shall shortly turn, is also used to express a point of view about the proper incidence of the responsibilities to which we have just referred. To say that someone is involuntarily unemployed is to relieve him of the responsibility for his condition; it is to suggest that he is unemployed 'through no fault of his own'; and, further, that if the individual is not responsible for his condition, then the state (rather than, say, the Salvation Army) must be.[1] In this way, government responsibility may be presented as coextensive with that part of unemployment that is involuntary; if individuals are voluntarily unemployed, then that is evidently their own business.

But at the same time as purporting to delimit the sphere of government responsibility, this category is also, as has been observed, intended to serve as a diagnostic tool. Involuntary unemployment arises because of a malfunctioning of the economic *system*: it is not that the individuals involved lack the willingness or ability to work, but rather that the economy is failing to provide them with the opportunity to do so.

With its popularisation by Keynes, the distinction between voluntary and involuntary unemployment became superimposed on the already widely adopted classification of unemployment into frictional, seasonal, cyclical and structural components.[2] As a result of the development of Keynesian ideas, however, the category of 'cyclical unemployment' was replaced by 'demand-deficient unemployment', partly, one supposes, in recognition of the possibility that even cycle peaks may not correspond to 'full employment' (or '100 per cent capacity utilization').

The question arises of whether the 'voluntary' versus 'involuntary' distinction adds anything further to the previously existing classification. Just what is it that is 'involuntary' about it? Is 'involuntary unemployment' just another name for 'demand-deficient unemployment', the Keynesian descendant of 'cyclical unemployment'?[3] Keynes's definition in his *General Theory* (1936, p. 15) seems to make it no more than that. Keynes says that workers are involuntarily unemployed if a small fall in the real wage, when brought about by a small rise in the price level (of wage-goods), results in both the demand for and supply of labour increasing beyond the existing volume of employment. Although the precise import of this definition is not immediately clear, it certainly means that Keynes was not envisaging workers in the aggregate supplying labour services in accordance with a standard upward-sloping supply curve. In fact it is hard to see why Keynes mentions labour supply at all, for the import of his definition is not that the supply of labour behaves perversely, but rather that it is irrelevant to the processes by which employment is determined. (Simple Keynesian models make labour supply irrelevant to employment determination; more elaborate ones allow it to play an indirect role in influencing the gradual adjustment of money wages.) The only role that the labour supply function plays in the Keynesian short-run, however, is to determine, as a residual, the volume of unemployment. The practice of carrying out analysis with labour 'off its supply curve' is, of course, simply another way of expressing the presumption of the involuntariness of this behaviour, transposed now from the individual to the market level.

The questions that we wish to raise here about the category 'involuntary unemployment' are: Can it be isolated empirically? Can it be given a theoretical rationalisation within some wider framework of ideas? What is its role in the analysis and evaluation of macroeconomic policies?

Work on the empirical issue is, as Standing (1981) has argued, exceedingly difficult to interpret in a conclusive way. A study sponsored by the Department of Health and Social Security and the Department of Employment, for example, tried to discriminate between voluntary and involuntary unemployment (Hill, 1976). The study used interviews with a sample of unemployed men in 1971. The only meaning the investigators were able to give to voluntary unemployment involved the judgement that those concerned might have tried harder to find a job: 'What is required ... is a value judgement about the amount of effort individuals should make in order to overcome their disadvantages and handicaps' (Hill, 1976, p. 183). From the point of view of welfare economics and economic policy, however, this is hardly helpful, for the amount of effort that should (in an allocative sense) be put into job-seeking is something that comes out of the problem, given the circumstances and the way the problem is formulated – it is not something that can be imposed *a priori*. The upshot of this study is accordingly that, whether or not there exists, at the purely conceptual level, a clear distinction between voluntary and involuntary unemployment, the distinction has so far eluded empirical implementation.[4]

In order to isolate what, in principle, is involuntary about involuntary unemployment, it is evident that one must give some attention to the relevant choices of labour market participants.[5] When one embarks on choice theory, however, one is focusing all one's attention precisely on the voluntariness of the behaviour in question. Accordingly, from a choice theory perspective, the prisoner pressing his face against the bars of his cell is doing exactly what he wants to do, given the constraints of his choice problem; similarly, the motorist who skids off the road and over the edge of a cliff was, given his limited knowledge of the consequences of alternative courses of action available to him, doing exactly as he wished. To adopt a choice-theoretic perspective is, therefore, to take all limitations on choice as *given*, as part of the individual's circumstances.

The difficulty of the task of giving a coherent and convincing choice-theoretic account of involuntary unemployment, however, may be taken in either of two ways: it may be taken as reflecting on the concept to be clarified or on the method by which clarification is sought. Thus, taking the latter alternative, if the idea of involuntary unemployment cannot be made to emerge from the logic of choice in the labour market, then that may be seen as a deficiency of the choice-logic approach to the problem. On this view we should simply hold fast to the concept of involuntary unemployment, and disregard any framework that cannot accommodate it, as Solow (1980a, p. 3, emphasis added) is doing when he writes: 'I believe that what looks like involuntary unemployment *is* involuntary unemployment'.[6] Standing (1981, p. 576) is expressing the same sentiment when he writes:

In ordinary discourse and in economic research there should be a basic presumption that if someone says he wants employment he should be regarded as involuntarily unemployed unless it is proved otherwise. In a sense, like anyone faced with a charge, he should be presumed innocent until proved guilty.

It is evident, however, that analytical ideas will not be clarified by the fiat of adopted conventions and presumptions. In order to make any progress analytically, it is necessary to give some attention to the way, or the variety of ways, in which the unemployed state may be brought to an end. We must address the question, in other words, of what manner of thing an employment opportunity (or 'job') is.

How does one conceive of an 'employment opportunity'? First of all, it is not the same thing as a vacancy, since an employment opportunity may consist of becoming self-employed. But there is an issue, quite apart from that, in how we think about such things. At one extreme, we can think in physical terms, along the following lines. Productive activity requires capital equipment in order to carry it out; therefore the creation of capital creates 'jobs': it provides people with the equipment with which to work. Of course, this approach overlooks (or regards as obviously soluble) the problem of ensuring that investment is well-directed. It also fails to recognise the substitutability between labour and capital (although with embodied technology and non-malleable capital, the idea can be rescued). All this aside, however, it is an important strand of thought, especially on the political Left. Put at its crudest, it allows the blame for unemployment to be put on capitalists for their failure to invest, and the onus to fill the deficiency in investment to be put on the state.

At the other extreme, one could think about employment opportunities in much the same way that Austrian economists think about profit opportunities: not as something objectively 'there', but as something in the eye of the beholder. This would put more emphasis than is customary on the possibilities for self-employment; but apart from that, there are many possibilities for the display of entrepreneurial qualities in the search for employment in a wage- or salary-earning capacity (although it may well be that these qualities are displayed far more by those already-employed individuals who are seeking better employment opportunities than by the unemployed).

Suppose an individual finds himself unemployed (for whatever reason). There are various ways in which he might become re-employed:

(1) by lowering his aspirations (taking a job of a kind he was not previously prepared to take, or at a wage he was previously not prepared to accept – note that the former process can operate perfectly well even if wages are 'rigid');
(2) by acquiring new skills (this takes time; also, since many skills are acquired on the job, this may not be possible; what he has to acquire are the characteristics that betoken on-the-job trainability, or trainability at low cost);
(3) by intensive search (including the decision to widen the scope of search – so overlapping with (1) and perhaps (2) above);
(4) by becoming self-employed. Of course, by becoming self-employed one ceases in a purely definitional or classificatory sense to be unemployed. But from a substantive point of view, the self-employed may still be unemployed (or underemployed). (From the point of view of demand deficiency, of course, a switch to self-employment would be no help.)

The categories on this list are intended to be neither exhaustive nor mutually exclusive. The object is rather to give some idea of the possibilities for an individual to become employed as a result of his own efforts. As we may see from even this cursory discussion, the efforts involved are a matter of engaging in *activities*: of reconsidering one's aspirations; of training and of acquiring skills; of searching (within a particular range of markets); of reconsidering the scope of one's search activities; and so on. One's desire for employment will be manifest in the intensity with which one engages in these activities. At this level of practicality, then, becoming employed is not just a matter of making a *decision*: whether to accept employment or not on given terms. Rather, it is a matter of engaging ('investing') in the appropriate activities.

Someone who didn't plant seeds is presumably 'voluntarily' without plants that he could have cultivated. But suppose someone plants seeds which fail to grow because he, as it happens, doesn't give them enough water or fertilizer. Is he then 'voluntarily' without the plants? More to the point: is the question worth bothering with? Although one may be able to assemble a set of conventions such as to enable this category to be applied in some cases and not in others, it seems hard to imagine its having any horticultural interest beyond suggesting, perhaps, that we should not waste our sympathy on those would-be gardeners who are 'voluntarily' without plants. Similarly with those who are without employment. One could, as Standing (1981) does, propose a set of conventions such that the presumption is always in favour of the unemployment being seen as involuntary; the force of this would then be that those concerned should always be given the benefit of the doubt as candidates for our sympathy.

As has been mentioned already, the putative 'involuntariness' of the behaviour involved where unemployed persons fall within this category, may be considered either at the level of individual market decisions or at the level of market aggregates. Indeed, as soon as we address the issue of whether the various (intended) market decisions of individual agents may in fact all be realised in the aggregate, we are brought face to face with the question of the relationship between these two levels of analysis, a topic that we evidently must pursue.

The counterpart, at the market level, of 'involuntariness' at the level of individuals, is 'disequilibrium'. There is therefore an analytical problem of explaining how the state of market disequilibrium can lead to (or be associated with) this involuntariness on the part of individuals. Once this connection has been clarified, we should be able to see whether the equilibrium versus disequilibrium debate is simply the voluntary versus involuntary issue transposed from the individual to the market level.

Suppose, for reasons unspecified, that the real wage is too high for market clearing. What this means, putting it another way, is that there are households that would like to sell more labour than they are doing at this ruling wage, but find themselves unable to do so. What it also means is that there are employers who are paying higher wages than they 'really need to' (given the underlying market conditions). The problem for disequilibrium theory (and for the associated idea of involuntary unemployment as anything more than a manifestation of the turbulence of a large or unaccustomed adjustment process) is then to explain how the frustrated would-be sellers of labour and the presumably disgruntled buyers of labour at above the rate consistent with underlying market conditions do not do what is in their common interest, namely, trade at a real wage lower than the prevailing one, and thereby contribute to a reduction in its overall level. What needs to be addressed, therefore, is the problem of how to explain or, at least, to model, the persistence of disequilibrium states (in the sense of non-clearing markets). Putting this another way round, the problem is to explain the 'stickiness' of wages (or the inertia that is manifest in gradual wage/price adjustment).

The accounts that have been offered of this phenomenon may be divided into two schools. The first account has its origins in the work of Clower (1965), and has been greatly elaborated by Leijonhufvud (1968, 1973). The second account is one that has been popularised by Malinvaud (1977) and that has its origins in the work of the French School of which Malinvaud is a prominent member. For ease of exposition, however, I shall label the two accounts with the names of Clower and Malinvaud alone. Their accounts could be summarised as follows:

(1) *Clower.* Non-clearing market states have certain self-reinforcing tendencies (which is not to say that they do not also have any self-correcting tendencies). These self-reinforcing tendencies may offset the self-correcting tendencies or, at any rate, impede their operation. There is also a presumption that these self-reinforcing ('deviation-amplifying' as Leijonhufvud (1968) calls them) processes will be stronger when the departure from market-clearing is large, abrupt, in an unfamiliar direction, or pervasive (Leijonhufvud, 1973). Thus, there is nothing in Clower's idea to explain how an economy gets into a disequilibrium state in the first place; it is concerned only with the consequences of being in such a state and the resulting difficulty in getting out of one, however it may have been arrived at.

(2) *Malinvaud.* Here the idea is that other arrangements may arise to fulfil the function that relative prices would otherwise carry out. Thus, if the rationing of goods is not brought about by the adjustment of relative prices, there may be other procedures or arrangements ('non-price

rationing', e.g. queues) by means of which goods are rationed between agents. It is then the existence of such arrangements that takes the pressure off relative prices: these arrangements mean that excess demands need not manifest themselves as a pressure on relative prices but rather, for example, as a lengthening of queues.[7]

Both of these lines of thought are evidently susceptible of great elaboration. For the purpose of the present discussion, however, it is sufficient to appreciate that each arises from addressing the issue that agents involved in a system of non-clearing markets will not have any clear idea of the equilibrium state implicit in current circumstances, and so will have to base their decisions on the information and incentives actually generated by the prevailing state of affairs. The essential point is that such incentives and the information they embody are – not at all surprisingly – far less reliable guides to reaching the state of general compatibility of trading plans than the information and incentives generated by that state itself, if it were achieved. (Thus, as is recounted by general equilibrium theorists, an idealised auctioneer could, by sufficiently systematic interrogation of traders concerning their contingent plans, and the pooling of the (assumed truthful) answers, provide all the co-ordination that is needed to avoid completely this floundering; by avoiding the floundering, it would thereby be possible to avoid any effect that the floundering process would have had on economic circumstances and hence on the state of general market-clearing implicit in those circumstances.)

What is more important for the present discussion than the elaboration of the implications of the modelling of non-clearing market states is the fundamental supposition of the whole approach. This is that employment, in conditions of excess supply of labour, is determined by the demand for it, and impervious to the supply. As Robert Hall (1980, p. 237, emphasis in original) has put it:

The model implicit in most Keynesian work says that prices and wages are sticky *and* that labor demand, not labor supply, determines employment (this is certainly true in the basic IS-LM model). In the Keynesian story, the labor market operates off the labor supply function, for reasons which so far have not been successfully explained. It is not enough just to invoke the practical reality that wages and prices are sticky. We need to explain why demand wins and supply loses in the contest to determine employment in the face of stickiness.

Thus, these discussions of disequilibrium states and what happens in them do not provide any explanation of why labour is off its supply curve, or why what happens is entirely adapted to what firms want to do. Rather, the discussions are addressed to working out the possible expenditure implications of taking it for granted that these things will be so. So, although such discussion is often spoken of as dealing with 'market failure' (at a highly aggregative level), it should be seen that the discussion does not contribute towards any explanations of why or how markets are failing. Rather, the explanations are concerned to explore some possible income and expenditure implications of markets failing in a particular manner.

The discussion of involuntary unemployment as a manifestation of some manner of failure of a system of interdependent markets naturally raises the question of the standards by which success or failure of such a system is to be judged. Thus, if a market system is failing, it must be doing so either relative to some 'ideal' (or even 'satisfactory') mode of functioning, or relative to the mode of functioning of some alternative way in which the system could be organised: that is, markets supplemented or replaced by administrative machinery and political activities. Accordingly, any discussion of market failure goes hand in hand with a parallel discussion of its correction by government action. Indeed, it is possible to take the need for government intervention, rather than the condition that warrants it, as the defining characteristic of involuntary unemployment, as Trygve Haavelmo (1950) has proposed. Haavelmo's proposal is accordingly to say that unemployment is 'involuntary' if it requires a *collective* choice to remove it. Unfortunately, however, Haavelmo provides no discussion of the costs and informational requirements of collectively made decisions (as compared with their individually made alternatives) to reduce unemployment. Accordingly, his reliance on the notion that there are problems that 'require' collective decisions for their solution is, from the standpoint of the present discussion, entirely question-begging. The idea, however, of there being political and administrative procedures that provide either an alternative or a supplement to the decentralised processes of individual decision-making by which employment may be generated, is one which surely merits further attention. Thus, it is well recognised that there need be no unemployment problems *within* a collectivity organised along strictly hierarchical lines. Barbara Wootton (1938, pp. 237–8), for example, has observed: 'there is never any problem of unemployment in any group in which the market has been eliminated altogether: such, for example, as a monastery or an army. In such communities as these the distribution [i.e. allocation] of time and resources may indeed be very wastefully managed; but no one ever suffers from wanting work and being unable to find it.'

One way in which we may pursue the role of collective action in remedying unemployment problems is to consider the clear-cut case in which the labour market is completely collectivised. We may do this by supposing that the entire labour force is employed by the state; everyone wishing to work presents himself to the Ministry of Labour and is automatically accepted, as of right; the Ministry of Labour then decides what job each individual shall carry out and what pay goes with it. In such a system there would, of course, be no involuntary unemployment; instead, however, what would have happened is that the *content* of employment has become involuntary. This extreme case does make it clear, though, that it is always possible, by a sufficiently drastic form of collective action, to ensure that everyone who wants a job can have one, provided that all concerned either sacrifice, or have taken away from them, the right to choose which job it shall be. It is evident, therefore, that what is involved in 'the market' being 'eliminated altogether' within a group is that those joining the group either relinquish, or have taken from them, all freedom of choice in the matter of what labour services they shall perform, as between alternative available tasks.

If, therefore, following Haavelmo, we propose to distinguish involuntary unemployment by a comparison between the functioning of a market system on the one hand and, on the other hand, some political and administrative alternative to it, we must take care, in doing so, to make the appropriate comparisons. It would be pointless to characterise unemployment generated by the (imperfect) workings of actual markets as 'involuntary' on the grounds that it would be avoidable by the intervention of some 'ideal' (omniscient and benevolent) *deus ex machina* labelled 'the government'. This would be just as pointless as saying that unemployment is 'voluntary' if it could be eliminated by the functioning of an 'ideal' market system. The functioning of either 'ideal' markets or 'ideal' governments is of little interest to those who find themselves unemployed as a result of the combined functioning of actual markets as modified by the intervention of actual governments. But following the logic of this discussion leads to the conclusion that Haavelmo's proposal is thoroughly unhelpful, for the proposal requires that we need to know exactly how the workings of markets (and labour markets in particular) may be improved, guided and reformed by the introduction of administrative machinery and the commitment to political action, even before we can diagnose the extent to which the unemployment is 'involuntary' (i.e. susceptible to that remedy). If the only way in which we could recognise the common cold is by its responsiveness to treatments for the common cold, there would hardly be any point in making the distinction between diagnosis and treatment. The situation would be made especially futile by the fact that, not being able to recognise common colds except through their treatment, we could never be in a position to know whether a particular treatment was effective or ineffective *as a cold treatment*: conditions that responded to the treatment may, for all we know, not have been common colds; and, *vice versa*, conditions that failed to respond may have been common colds after all. In summary, then, a diagnostic test is useful only in so far as it may be applied independently of the results of the treatment for the condition so diagnosed. It is on this criterion that the Haavelmo proposal founders.

The possibility of government action to improve the working of a market system emerges as soon as we consider the manner in which such a system may malfunction. Once, however, we begin to inquire according to what standards of functioning we recognise 'malfunctioning', the whole issue becomes both complex and contentious. The mere fact that the system happens to be functioning away from some analytically specified general equilibrium state (i.e. that prices are 'sticky' and do not adjust instantaneously to a general market-clearing configuration) is really neither here nor there when it comes to assessing the relative merits of alternative political and administrative arrangements for promoting the smooth co-ordination of activities. As Robert Barro (1979, p. 55) has remarked:

> Presumably, sticky wages or prices are not intended to be taken literally as the source of private sector inefficiency. The underlying problem must reflect some deeper economic elements, such as imperfect information about the present or future, factor mobility costs, or some types of significant transaction costs. Although some of these elements are probably important in business cycle analyses, it is not apparent that they imply relative efficiency of the government over the private sector in handling such economic disturbances as oil crises, harvest failures, or even autonomous changes in liquidity preference or the perceived marginal product of capital – if such shifts occur on a significant scale. For example, uncertainty and mobility costs seem to imply that the allocation of resources is a difficult problem – not that the government can assist in allocation through active use of its macro-policy instruments.

3.   The pragmatics of 'demand deficiency'

Within the Keynesian system, the existence of involuntary unemployment is taken as a symptom of a condition of demand deficiency within the economy. One way in which we may hope to elucidate the concept of involuntary unemployment, therefore, is by a discussion of how, and in relation to what, demand may be deficient. Since, however, this diagnostic use of the concept is intended to be of practical relevance in the guidance of policy, it will be appropriate to discuss the concept in the context of just such a practical, policy-oriented concern.

Once we begin to think pragmatically about demand deficiency, however, further questions arise. First there is the question of whether it is real or nominal demand that we are talking about. It is nominal demand that can be modified by policy actions. But if the deficiency is in real demand, then to speak of a deficiency presupposes that a change in nominal demand will not lead (or will not immediately lead) to a proportional increase in the price (and wage) level. The practical issue that underlies the notion of demand deficiency is therefore the extent to which, and the speed with which, an increase in real demand engineered by the authorities may be offset by a rising wage and price level. Accordingly, this pragmatic perspective on demand expansion leads quickly to the conclusion that an understanding of demand deficiency depends on an appreciation of the repercussions – especially on costs and prices – of engineering an expansion in aggregate demand.

Once one has arrived at the conclusion that changes in aggregate demand cannot be engineered as isolated effects, the question arises as to whether one can give analytical or statistical expression to the connection between demand pressure, on the one hand, and, on the other hand, its repercussions. The Phillips curve in its various manifestations is one answer to this question. Specifically, it says that costs respond to aggregate demand expansion because wage inflation will respond to the lower level of unemployment corresponding to the higher pressure of demand. In times when it was still possible to believe that the (simple) Phillips curve gave a reasonably adequate picture of these repercussions, it was natural to incorporate it into a discussion of demand-deficient unemployment, an exercise carried out by Lipsey (1968). (A similar exercise was also carried out by Samuelson and Solow, 1960).

In his article Lipsey was concerned with the implications of the Phillips curve for the distinction between demand-deficient (Lipsey calls it 'deficient demand') and other unemployment (structural and frictional). His basic point is that, with a negatively sloped Phillips curve, there is no limit to the amount of unemployment that can be removed by demand expansion: the only thing one can say is that removing increasing amounts becomes increasingly costly in terms of its inflationary consequences. But this means that a classification of unemployment in terms of either causes or remedies has broken down. All that remains is a classification by the relative costliness of reducing the unemployment by one means or another. Demand-deficient unemployment is simply that part of unemployment that is less costly to remove by demand expansion than by other means ('improving the working of labour markets'). But this surely makes the classification nebulous to the point of invisibility: one might as well admit that the classification has dissolved.

The kind of exercise carried out by Lipsey can be taken in either of two ways. On the surface, it appears to be a constructive venture, providing an analytical basis for discriminating between 'demand-deficient' and other kinds of unemployment. But when one considers that in order to do this one has to have a stable (over time and in the face of macro-policy changes) Phillips curve with an appreciable negative slope and also a set of well-defined (and presumably stable) social indifference curves, one begins to wonder about the upshot of the exercise. Is it, perhaps, that the concept of demand deficiency is the product of an income/expenditure model with only a single target of policy: a level of real income (assumed to correspond to a particular level of capacity utilization and, perhaps, also of unemployment); that the concept cannot survive outside the artificial environment of that simple world; and that it is easy prey to any second, conflicting target of policy that may happen along?

An individual may become employed as a result of action by the state (Haavelmo's 'collective choice'). Thus the government can, in a sense 'create jobs'; but it is important to appreciate in what sense (or in what circumstances) it can do this. Just what these limitations are is a fiercely contested issue, and is at the heart of the dispute between monetarists and Keynesians. This issue does need to be raised, however, in order to set up the appropriate comparisons when we think about the possibilities for employment of an unemployed individual. Thus:

(1)   he may become employed through his own efforts;
(2)   he may become employed as a result of action by the state.

(This is not at all a clean dichotomy. Even with state action, the individual will still need to make *some* effort in order to become employed, although it will be less than would have been required otherwise.)

Each of these kinds of effort will have costs. Not only will there be costs associated with the efforts of the unemployed individual and the efforts of the state (and the repercussions thereof), but also there may be costs of an allocative kind if the employment found in one case is more productive than in the other. What is suggested by this line of development is the possibility that involuntary unemployment be identified with unemployment the removal of which is (in some sense) less costly by the state than for the individuals concerned by their own efforts. But to allow this identification would be to abandon any notion of involuntariness being involved (although wouldn't this formulation perhaps capture rather better what those who talk about involuntary unemployment have in mind?). Classification, however, is in the nature of a preliminary business: we classify things *first*, before going on to further inquiry. But if the ability to classify depends on intricate comparisons of the cost of alternative kinds of state and individual actions (and their consequences) then it can emerge only as the conclusion of an elaborate inquiry. The classification ceases to have anything to do with the *state* of the unemployed individual or the *cause* of that state; it refers only to the relationship between the costs of alternative remedies.

4. Demand deficiency in its cyclical context

If demand is deficient, it must be deficient in relation to something. That something is presumably the level of costs. So, with greater strictness, what we are talking about is 'a deficiency of demand in relation to costs', which can be thought of quite equivalently as 'an excess of costs in relation to demand'. It is natural, however, to focus on whichever item in the comparison is felt to be the more malleable: we talk of a 'deficiency of demand' on the tacit assumption that demand is more malleable than costs are. The case for conceiving of matters in this way therefore centres on the obstacles to the general reduction of costs (and especially wage costs).

The basis for regarding unemployment as a symptom of 'deficient demand' rather than 'excess costs' must accordingly be that aggregate demand is believed to be more malleable than costs; that is, that a given degree of adjustment of demand relative to costs is, in some sense, thought to be less costly to achieve through an increase in demand than through a reduction in costs. From this point of view, all talk of 'involuntariness' would seem to be a complete red herring. Since, however, this reasoning depends not just on the malleability of demand, but on the malleability (via demand expansion) of the relationship between demand and costs, it rests, in this formulation, on the assumption of the relative unresponsiveness of costs to demand pressures, and especially the unresponsiveness of wage costs to demand pressures. It may occur, though, as is perhaps too familiar to need pointing out, that the effects of demand expansion are rapidly undermined by cost increases. There is, of course, a highly contentious matter of the extent to which such costs increases should be seen as *repercussions* of the expansionary measures (operating either through labour market pressures or through international trade and payments and thereby exchange rates and import prices) or as (largely) autonomous developments. To preserve a basis for 'demand deficiency' one has to take the latter view, for otherwise one admits that demand is, after all, not malleable *relative to costs*.

If one does take this latter view, one can conclude, with G. D. N. Worswick (1977, p. 16), that: 'The lesson of the past is not that demand management did not work. It did – but it was not enough. The point is not to discard it but to buttress it with additional instruments.' What this means in plain English is that as well as pushing up on demand, the government should press down on costs. But in what sense is the government then practising 'demand management' rather than 'cost management' or even 'profitability management'? The line of reasoning exemplified by this quote from Worswick leads to the unhelpful conclusion that demand expansion will have its effect on real output and employment provided only that it is prevented from having an effect on anything else.

But this talk of 'buttressing with additional instruments' is not only unhelpful, it is also disingenuous. For, given enough buttressing, anything can be achieved: if the central government authorities are in a position to write a script for the whole economic drama, then they can make sure that it conforms to their prevailing idea of an edifying overall plot, and one in which the supporting characters never have a chance to upstage the stars. But this leaves unasked and unanswered a number of politically contentious questions concerning just how much power is, could be and should be concentrated in the hands of the central authorities of government. Indeed, this way of looking at the matter has the result that the degree of centralisation of economic power is allowed to emerge as a residual from the solution to problems of macroeconomic management. The implication is that one just goes on concentrating and centralising power until one has enough of it to carry out counter-cyclical employment policies. As a manifestation of impatience and frustration in the face of the apparent imperviousness of the economy to the policies to which it is supposed – according to the previously prevailing orthodoxy – to respond, this attitude is understandable. But as an exercise in political economy, it succeeds in providing an approach to macroeconomic issues only by treating with the utmost carelessness the rather fundamental issue of the appropriate balance in the economy between the centralisation and decentralisation of power.

Pursuit of these issues would soon take the discussion very far afield indeed. For our present purposes, however, the issue that needs to be addressed is the fact that when we talk about policies that influence demand and costs, and about the malleability or autonomy of those aggregates, we are discussing variables that are, in any case, exhibiting fluctuations. Within the income/expenditure model, the procedure is to think not of fluctuations as such, but rather of a succession of states of affairs, any one of which may be singled out for individual analysis. This device, however, is not without its risks and difficulties, just as, in the study of mechanics, when the motion of a particle is thought of as its successively occupying a sequence of adjacent positions, one risks facing the question whether, in 'occupying' each position, the particle is 'instantaneously at rest' rather than in the state of motion in which one had originally understood it to be. As is possible in mechanics, these deep problems may be brushed aside in so far as one is prepared to think in terms of states of suspended animation. Indeed, Keynesian economics has gone further than that in its willingness to suspend animation: it has persistently set itself the task of presenting the unemployment associated with a deep and protracted recession (and perhaps with any recession?) as being an 'under-employment *equilibrium*'. The development of Keynesian ideas – that is, the development of their analytical expression – has accordingly resulted in 'demand deficiency' becoming an essentially static idea in which the cyclical context of demand and employment fluctuations is either disregarded or, at best, is left out of focus in the middle distance.

Despite the analytical convenience of this device, the object of the exercise is to provide guidance in the formulation of policies to counteract a major component of those fluctuations. Accordingly, the analytical results that follow from the income/expenditure model are in need of re-animation to bring them back into contact with policy problems. There is therefore a job of work to be done in putting 'demand deficiency' back into the cyclical context from which it has been extracted. This task has been carried out by Robert Lucas Jr. (1977).

His argument proceeds as follows:

(1)   Chapter 1 of Keynes's *General Theory* should be read as a declaration that 'unemployment was not explainable as a consequence of individual choices and that failure of wages to move as predicted by the classical theory was to be treated as due to forces beyond the powers of economic theory to illuminate' (Lucas, 1977, pp. 11–12).[8]

(2)   '...' by simply sidestepping this problem with the unexplained postulate of rigid nominal prices, an otherwise classical model would be transformed into a model which did a fair job of accounting for observed time series' (Lucas, 1977, p. 12).

On this account, Keynes did not have any explanation for unemployment; his model, however, has the pragmatic justification that, by avoiding this question altogether, it somehow generates results in conformity with some aspects of observed cyclical patterns (for example, the pro-cyclical behaviour of investment and nominal interest rates). If, however, one were to take the *General Theory* at its face value as a theory of employment, and hence unemployment, there is no reason why one should not inquire exactly what is the explanation it offers for these phenomena. But if, as Lucas argues – correctly, in my view – Keynes's model has its pragmatic success precisely by sidestepping this issue, then to reintroduce the issue that had to be sidestepped is going to produce trouble: the literature on the 'micro-foundations of macro-economics' is testimony to just how debilitating this trouble can be when reintroduced, even when one sets oneself the relatively modest task of providing an analytical niche for cyclical unemployment in its 'suspended animation' guise. What the Keynesian framework gives us, therefore, in the absence of a developed explanation for cyclical unemployment, is a model that is nevertheless consistent with some of the stylised facts of the cyclical co-variation. As some of the variables involved are subject to control or influence by government authorities, this sets the stage for action. It means that we have a basis for attempting to move from one kind of cyclical state to another, without having to understand why we were in the initial state in the first place. But the success of this attempt depends, of course, on the stylised cyclical pattern being maintained in the face of its being used as the fulcrum of policy leverage: the cyclical pattern needs to be invariant with respect to arbitrary alternative time paths of policy variables, over the relevant range of variation. If the cyclical patterns break down (as a result of policy leaning too hard on them, or for whatever reason) then the policy will come unstuck.

The point is that, as we have seen, the transition from 'cyclical' to 'demand-deficient' unemployment depends on wholly pragmatic considerations. There may be circumstances in which the transition is justified. Just how little we know about the range of such circumstances is one of the more painful lessons of the 1970s. Given the wholly pragmatic basis for using 'demand deficiency' as a diagnostic tool, it is entirely appropriate that, whenever the diagnosis appears not to be working, we should be prepared to abandon it and reconsider the particular conjunction of circumstances in which cyclical movements are taking place.

5. Concluding Remarks

We have seen that 'demand deficiency' arises as the counterpart, at the aggregate level, of the 'involuntary unemployment' of individuals. Its rationale, as a diagnostic category, therefore depends either on our ability to provide an adequate account of how we recognise when − or the extent to which − individuals are 'involuntarily unemployed'; or, failing that, it would depend, somewhat more precariously, on our ability to formulate aggregative models in which, brushing aside or taking for granted its 'microeconomic' rationale, the notion of demand deficiency may be given a clear meaning. In so far as the whole exercise is intended to have a bearing on the design and conduct of macroeconomic policies, the diagnostic value of the category of demand deficiency would evidently depend on such aggregative models being sufficiently robust in operation to maintain their structure in the face of turbulence and policy changes; and also sufficiently rich to permit the expression of policy problems as they are currently understood.

The early sections of this paper were concerned with the search for a rationale for the concept of 'involuntary unemployment'. The thrust of this discussion was that the 'involuntariness' of individual behaviour could be rationalised only via some notion of 'market failure'; this 'market failure', in turn, required elucidation in terms of the alternative political and administrative arrangements whereby the same ends might be more efficiently achieved. But pursuit of the question of the relative efficiency of these alternatives led rapidly into a proliferation of questions, on the face of it, about their costs and informational requirements: questions, ultimately, of political will, legislative skill and administrative competence: questions that need to be answered – or evaded – before one can properly apply the category of 'involuntary unemployment'. The conclusion that emerges is therefore that the category of involuntary unemployment becomes usable provided we already know what is the most efficient way to manage the economy in general and the labour market in particular. But, as the purpose of the category is to help us, from a state in which that understanding is lacking, to move towards its attainment, it evidently becomes usable at exactly the same point at which it becomes unnecessary. It becomes usable at just that point at which we know what it is supposed to help us to find out; but not before.

In the later sections of this chapter, we have considered 'demand deficiency' as an aggregative category independently of whether it can be provided with an adequate 'microeconomic' rationale. It has been noted that within the most basic species of income/expenditure model, this notion of 'demand deficiency' may be given an unambiguous meaning. It has been pointed out, however, that such models evade certain questions concerning the malleability (by policy) and the autonomy (in the face of turbulence and policy changes) of key aggregates, a cluster of questions that have been grouped together and discussed under the heading of the 'the pragmatics of "demand deficiency"'. The central issues here were isolated as being the malleability of aggregate demand (relative to something that must be comparatively unresponsive to demand pressures) and the autonomy of costs (this latter being represented in the income/expenditure framework as either the exogeneity of all prices; or, less restrictively, the exogeneity of money wages; or, less restrictively still, the gradual adjustment of prices and wages). It was suggested, as a result of this discussion, that the clarity of the concept of demand deficiency was entirely dependent on the absence of any conflicting objective of macro-policy: for if demand is 'deficient' with respect to one objective, but 'excessive' with respect to another, what can one say?

It was then argued that the pursuit of these pragmatic considerations leads one inexorably back to the cyclical context from which the notion of 'demand deficiency' – seen as a property of an 'under-employment *equilibrium*' – had been extracted. The conclusion here is accordingly the somewhat depressing one that it has taken us forty or fifty years to come full circle: we have now, I think, retrieved the appreciation that the business cycle is an exceedingly puzzling phenomenon, and not something the control of which is a matter of the application of fiscal brute force, nor of policies the application of which is precluded only by the prevalence, in high places, of financial dogma and obscurantism.

Notes to Chapter 3

1. Thus, Worswick (1976, p. 14) asks:

> Was this attempt [i.e. Keynes's] to distinguish involuntary and voluntary unemployment merely technical, or was it intended to raise issues of personal and social responsibility? When a man loses a job and cannot obtain another it may be his own fault; it is not difficult to recognise such cases. Equally it is not difficult to find instances where there is nothing the individual could do to prevent the loss of a job; we then say it was the fault of the economic and social system. The importance of the distinction is obvious. If the responsibility lies with the individual, social action to help him find another job may be desirable, but it is certainly not necessary. But if the loss of the job lies outside his own control, then only social [i.e. political?] action can provide any remedy. Was this what Keynes was after with his distinction?

2. Although the notion of 'involuntary unemployment' is commonly associated with the name of Keynes, its use pre-dates his work of the 1930s in which the term was popularised. The earliest instance of it that Richard Kahn (1976, p. 19) was able to track down was its use by Pigou in 1914. It was also used by Dennis Robertson (1915, p. 210) at the same time.

3. Samuel Brittan (1976, p. 259) claims that this is so when he writes:

The distinction between voluntary and involuntary unemployment is a 'micro' concept, applicable to the individual, and is a matter of degree. Keynes's 'involuntary unemployment' is far better labelled 'demand-deficient unemployment'. He quite clearly had in mind the kind of unemployment that could be cured by what he called in his 1937 *Times* article 'a general stimulus at the centre'. Presumably, the reason for his earlier insistence on the term 'involuntary unemployment' was to emphasise that demand deficiency could be an equilibrium condition – a doctrinal point which, to put it mildly, no longer seems very pressing.

4. Thus, Kahn (1976, p. 26) writes:

> the distinction between 'voluntary' and 'involuntary' unemployment, while important conceptually as a basis for the Keynesian system of analysis, has not proved to have any practical significance, either in terms of statistical measurement or in terms of targets and objectives.'

Kahn does not, however, explain to us how a distinction that 'has not proved to have any practical significance' can nevertheless remain 'important conceptually as a basis for the Keynesian system of analysis'.

5. As Patinkin (1965, pp. 313–4) discovered to his chagrin, however, the attempt may result in the whole idea slipping through one's fingers. Thus:

> In the absolute sense, the whole notion of 'involuntariness' must disappear: for everyone 'wants' to do whatever he is doing at the moment; otherwise he would not do it. It is only by comparing an individual's reactions under given circumstances with his corresponding reactions under arbitrarily designated 'ideal' circumstances that we are able to define the element of 'involuntariness' which may be involved. Thus our first task in defining 'involuntary unemployment' is to define that behaviour which is to be taken as the norm of voluntariness.

This instance of the attempt to accommodate the idea of 'involuntary unemployment' within a choice-theoretic framework is instructive, for, in effect, the whole idea of involuntariness is simply abandoned in favour of that of departure from some 'normal' or 'ideal' state of affairs, which is evidently not the same sort of idea at all.

6. Solow (1980b, p. 253) elaborates this view, elsewhere, as follows:

> It would be easy to produce a model in which prices adjust almost instantaneously to shocks, markets clear essentially all the time, and the correct policy is to do nothing. The trouble with such a model is that it fails so transparently to reflect any actual economy. It therefore has to be supplemented by an elaborate pretense that what looks like involuntary unemployment is really voluntary, that what looks like idleness is really investment in human capital, that what looks like excess supply is really an optimal response to some epidemic misperception of the current state of affairs. I suppose it is a step forward to convert transparent failure into opaque failure. Nevertheless, I shall ... analyse the consequences of supply shocks in a model in which prices move only slowly in response to disequilibrium, so that markets do not necessarily clear in a time period long enough for macroeconomic policy to be effective.

7. *Question*: Why have burglars stopped coming in through the front window?
   Answer 1: Because we have had window locks fitted (Clower).

Answer 2: Because the burglars have discovered that the back door is always open (Malinvaud).

8. In elaboration, Lucas (1977, p. 12) goes on as follows:

> Keynes wrote as though the 'involuntary' nature of unemployment were verifiable by direct observation, as though one could somehow look at a market and verify directly whether it is in equilibrium or not. Nevertheless, there were serious empirical reasons behind this choice, for nowhere is the 'apparent contradiction' between 'cyclical phenomena' and 'economic equilibrium' theory sharper than in labor market behaviour: Why, in the face of moderately fluctuating nominal wages and prices, should households *choose* to supply labor at sharply irregular rates through time? Most business cycle theorists had avoided this crucial problem, and those who addressed it had not resolved it.

Similarly, Karl Brunner (1971, pp. 35–6) has argued as follows:

> Keynes noted at the beginning of *The General Theory* that inherited price theory failed to explain mass unemployment. This failure actually went further. For inherited price theory failed to explain short-run variations in the rate of utilization of any resource and could not cope with the observed differences in the variability in such utilization rates. The income-expenditure approach was evolved in response to this intellectual crisis. It offered an explanation of the level and of variations in employment which essentially by-passed price theory. Its view centred on a (selected) flow of funds pushing and reacting on each other irrespective of relative price changes.

4

Deficient Foresight

1. Introduction

The fact that J. M. Keynes had made a distinguished contribution to the theory of probability (Keynes, 1921) no doubt predisposed many of his readers to imbue with great significance his subsequent remarks on the related topic of uncertainty in economic decision-making. Among those who have provided commentaries on his work, there are those who have singled out this uncertainty theme not only for its especial importance, but also for its potential for analytical subversion. The purpose of this chapter is to scrutinise the ideas involved in this particular aspect of Keynes's work, together with the lines of argument that have emerged from those commentators who have pursued it. The result of this scrutiny will be to call into question the idea that there is anything peculiarly subversive in the analytical consequences of broaching problems of uncertainty in economic decision-making. I shall argue, rather, that, as an analytical issue it is – depending on how it is handled – either innocuous or else quite indiscriminately destructive.

2. Keynes and uncertainty

Chapter 12 of Keynes's *General Theory*, 'The state of long-term expectation', deals with the knowledge of the future that would be required to make correct decisions regarding the instigation of capital projects. In particular, it revolves around the theme that, since infallible knowledge of the future is unattainable, the decisions to embark on capital projects must, in the nature of the case, be based on beliefs the epistemological foundations of which are more or less flimsy.[1] This chapter broaches, in other words, the theme of uncertainty in the making of investment decisions, a theme that makes a much brisker reappearance in Keynes's (1937) *Quarterly Journal of Economics* article which appeared shortly after his *General Theory*. This article is of especial importance in that it has been seized upon by a number of commentators on Keynes as providing the interpretative key to *The General Theory* and, indeed, to the whole tendency of his work of the 1930s, and perhaps even of his whole intellectual life.[2] The cogency of this interpretation is an issue that will be touched on (in connection with Hicks' views) in Chapter 5; the same issue will be taken up again in its own right in Chapter 6.

What is problematic about Keynes's discussion of uncertainty in the *QJE* article is the question of what its scope is supposed to be. On the face of it, the object of attention is economic activity in its entirety; specific categories of decision are mentioned – in particular, the decisions underlying private sector investment expenditure and the (stock) demand for liquid assets – but no reason is given why the considerations advanced should either be confined to these cases, or should apply with relatively greater consequence in these cases. Such differentiation, however, is precisely what would be required to sustain the argument that is being advanced, as I shall try to demonstrate in section 3 of this chapter.

As a matter of shorthand, it may be said, as many other commentators have done, that Keynes was, in the places referred to, broaching the theme of the *uncertainty* inherent in investment decisions. But although this is no doubt a convenient piece of shorthand, it fails to convey the root-and-branch quality of Keynes's discussion. For what Keynes is concerned to suggest is that the epistemological foundations of private sector investment are comprehensively flimsy. In elucidation of his conception of uncertainty, Keynes writes as follows (1937, p. 214):

> The sense in which I am using the term is that in which the prospect of a European war is uncertain, or the price of copper and the rate of interest twenty years hence, or the obsolescence of a new invention, or the position of private wealth-owners in the social system in 1970. About these matters there is no scientific basis on which to form any calculable probability whatever.

From the viewpoint of economic theory, however, this position is both odd and unhelpful. For, to paraphrase George Orwell: 'All expectations are uncertain; but some are more uncertain than others.' The price of copper twenty years hence is a thoroughly uncertain thing, and depends on so many circumstances the forecasting of which would be difficult and unreliable, that any one figure is, one might think, better seen as a guess than as anything more sophisticated. But it is worth pressing the example a bit further. For the belief, on any reasonable present understanding of the world, that the price of copper will, in 2002, be greater at 1982 prices than 10 cents per ton, and less than $1 billion per ton, is not at all uncertain. Pressing the example still further, it is even less uncertain that there will be a demand for copper in 2002; and even if this is to a degree uncertain (a hitherto undreamt-of copper substitute may be discovered, invented or developed) it is less uncertain that there will, in 2002, be a demand for metals of high electrical conductivity. And so on. Without pursuing the example any further, it should be apparent by now what I mean by the 'root-and-branch' aspect of Keynes's discussion. I shall return to this issue in section 4 of this chapter, where an attempt will be made to characterise in more detail just what is unsatisfactory about this approach to uncertainty in economic affairs.

3. The sources of variation in expenditure aggregates

At the period of time in which Keynes was working on the *General Theory*, the concept of 'the multiplier' – a means whereby autonomous variation in some category of expenditure could be transmitted, made pervasive and possibly amplified in its effects – had already been developed (Kahn, 1931). What Keynes needed to set his system in motion was a *source* of autonomous variation: some category of expenditure that is subject to fluctuations originating outside the model. As is well known, investment was the candidate chosen.

Investment decisions rest on beliefs about future circumstance, beliefs which in turn must be based on, if anything, present and past conditions. Accordingly, investment behaviour could exhibit erratic patterns if either:

(1) present conditions change erratically leading to erratically fluctuating beliefs about future circumstances; or
(2) beliefs change erratically without corresponding changes in their basis in conditions.

It is the second of these possibilities that leads to *autonomous* variations in the aggregate of expenditure resulting from investment decisions.

Accordingly, if changes in private investment have their origins in the spontaneous and erratic workings of individual minds, a solution to Keynes's problem is to hand: such an account provides the reason why this category of expenditure will fluctuate autonomously rather than in response to changes in objective circumstances (circumstances that should have their counterparts elsewhere in the model). It is in this way that subjectivist ideas make their appearance in Keynes's *General Theory*. These ideas have the effect of driving a wedge between behaviour and circumstances: they can be used, as it were, to detach behaviour from the circumstances in which it takes place. It should be noted, however, that the wedge is supposed to have its effect only on the behaviour of investors in the private sector of the economy.

This same wedge reappears in the theory of 'liquidity preference' as the means whereby wealth-holding decisions are given analytical autonomy, and whereby the rate of interest is thereby cut loose from economic 'circumstances'.[3] (Again, the application is evidently supposed to be restricted to the private sector of the economy.) For ease of exposition, attention has here been confined to the investment case, although the discussion could equally well be directed, *mutatis mutandis*, to that of liquidity preference.

It is worth emphasizing, in summary, that it is not the *fact* of uncertainty that is important for Keynes's argument, but rather how individuals are supposed to respond to the fact of uncertainty. Thus, if there is great uncertainty surrounding investment decisions, and producers respond to this by making, so far as is possible, the same investment decisions this period as last period (since, after all, the results of previous decisions are the one thing they do know something about), this would not result in private sector investment's being wayward and unruly; indeed, it might result in greater stability than would result from sophisticated calculations based on epistemologically privileged beliefs or an uncanny degree of foresight. Thus, the fact of uncertainty does not of itself establish the conclusion concerning the wayward and unruly behaviour of particular macroeconomic variables. Indeed, it is not even evident that this argument helps to establish Keynes's conclusion rather than the opposite conclusion.

Unless there is some way of restraining the application of these subjectivist ideas and their associated implications of uncertainty, they cannot serve the purpose that is required of them within Keynes's scheme. In that case they become merely an analytical red herring. For what is required within Keynes's scheme is not the uncertainty, as such, surrounding private sector investment decisions; it is the wayward and unruly behaviour of the aggregates resulting from the decisions taken in the face of this uncertainty. Indeed, Keynes's system requires private sector investment to display this unruliness in two quite distinct senses: first, when compared with private sector *consumer* expenditure (this is required in order for Keynes's model to work); and, second when compared with *public* sector investment expenditure (this is required in order for Keynes's policies to work). But since what is required is accordingly not the unruliness of private sector investment expenditure, but its *relative* unruliness when put into the context of the two comparisons to which we have just referred, it follows that, in the absence of some principle governing the relative influence of uncertainty on private versus public investment and on private investment versus private consumption (and hence saving), the uncertainty issue is, indeed, an analytical red herring. Given that the object of the exercise is to establish the relative unruliness of various expenditure aggregates, any discussion of pervasive, non-specific uncertainty is actually beside the point (even allowing – what we have in fact been disputing – that greater uncertainty surrounding the decisions would lead to greater unruliness in their outcomes over time). In the great stream of interpretation and appraisal, re-interpretation and re-appraisal of Keynes's work, this fact seems to have escaped attention.

Although subjectivist ideas do provide a wedge of sorts for driving between behaviour and circumstances, it is apparent that it is a thoroughly unwieldy tool with which to operate: it cannot be satisfactorily used in a selective and discriminating way to detach a certain class of behaviour (or the behaviour of a certain group of individuals) from the circumstances in which the behaviour takes place.

4. Certainty and fallibilism

What is unsatisfactory about focusing on the 'uncertainty' of expectations is its way of seeing knowledge and beliefs as falling so far short of some ideal state of certainty. If 'certainty' is interpreted in a way that makes it unattainable, why should we be interested in the lack of it? To assess beliefs by their uncertainty is like assessing one's progress on a journey not by how far one has travelled but by how far away the horizon is. The appropriate base line for assessing beliefs is ignorance, not omniscience. One may speculate on the progress that might have been made in geometry if the Greeks had succumbed to the temptation to measure distance by the extent to which it falls short of being infinite.

The state of certainty is in any case itself an ambiguous idea. For one could, firstly, regard certainty as a state of complete confidence in a belief, irrespective of whether that belief is correct (but how much confidence does one need for it to be 'complete'?); or one could regard it as a state of complete confidence in a belief together with the correctness of this belief and perhaps even the believer's having the grounds for entertaining the belief 'with certainty'.

Now, from the viewpoint of economic theory, the former concept of certainty as purely a state of 'complete' confidence is evidently not much use. Perfect confidence in a belief is perhaps far better sustained by ignorance than by understanding. And one would not feel at all happy expounding a theory in which everyone could – repeatedly – be perfectly confident one moment and discover themselves to have been wrong the next. So it is to the second idea of certainty as correct foresight that we are driven.

It is recognised that there are analytical difficulties with the concept of correct foresight. There are problems, notably, of how a number of interdependently acting individuals may simultaneously enjoy correct foresight. This is a theme on which

G. L. S. Shackle (1972) has dwelt at length, arguing that general and simultaneous correct foresight is possible only to the extent that the conditional plans and intentions of the individuals have been – somehow – 'pre-reconciled' within a state of general (market-clearing) equilibrium. This is an argument to which we shall return in Chapter 6. For the purposes of the present discussion, however, the point that needs to be made is that Shackle's argument can undoubtedly be rendered impregnable by the adoption of a sufficiently strong concept of market-clearing in which it is required, *inter alia*, that the expectations of agents are of a particular type and are fulfilled. What is less clear is whether such a way of proceeding is particularly helpful. For we may wish to recognise the fact that agents could become aware of the existence (or possibility) of non-clearing markets, and form expectations accordingly. The conditional plans that are pre-reconciled in the (Walrasian) kind of general equilibrium that Shackle evidently has in mind are plans each of which is made on the assumption that all markets *will* clear (that is, no one makes any plans for responding to 'trading difficulties'). But if the *form* of the expectations entertained by agents is restricted to this class, it is hardly surprising that they can be fulfilled only if a complete reconciliation is achieved, such as will avoid all the difficulties that – by the nature of the construction – the agents have disregarded in forming their expectations. If, however, the agents were allowed to form a wider range of plans, including plans conditional on the emergence of 'trading difficulties', then we have no reason at all to suppose that expectations of general market clearing are the only ones that are capable of being realised (that is, of being self-fulfilling in the aggregate, when acted upon). The pursuit of this line of argument, however, would take us into far deeper analytical waters than is necessary for our immediate purposes.

To say, as we did previously, that 'certainty' may be interpreted in a way that identifies it with some unattainable ideal, is, however, to gloss over the most important questions involved in deciding what one could reasonably mean by the term. Suppose that, proceeding along the lines of the preceding discussion, we were to provide an account of 'certainty' in terms of correct foresight. Suppose, moreover, that we were to start with the (as it will turn out, naïve) idea that foresight is correct if the future, when it arrives, *exactly* resembles what was foreseen, in every particular, at every instant. If that is what is meant by 'correct foresight', then its absence or non-attainment is a matter of utter triviality. But as soon as it is admitted that any *reasonable* conception of 'correct foresight' must allow for some (reasonable) margins of error, we are on the beginnings of a slippery slope. For we then have to admit that there is no clear dichotomy between certainty and uncertainty (or between knowledge and ignorance, for that matter). Just to emphasize this point, we could go to the other extreme and claim that all foresight is 'correct' (to some sufficiently lax standards of approximation), just as all foresight is 'incorrect' (by the absurd standards of comprehensive exactness).

Accordingly, suppose we reject as absurd the idea that 'correct foresight' is to be understood as foresight that is comprehensively exact in its correctness. We must then be driven to the notion that correctness must consist in the foresight's being within certain 'reasonable' bounds of approximation, and, as a development of this, of the scatter of actual cases within these bounds not exhibiting any *systematic* error. Accordingly, we may wish to insist that part of what we mean – or what we should mean – by 'correct foresight' is that the errors we make, even if they are all within the bounds of 'reasonable approximation' are not 'predominantly' in one direction: there are then further loose ends to be tidied up in elucidating what should count as 'predominantly' in one direction. As soon as one gets this far, it is evident that the notion of 'correct foresight' is crying out for statistical elaboration. It is very tempting to say that foresight is correct if the expected value of the error is zero. It is then a technical problem to devise tests to determine whether the expected value of the error in any particular case differs from zero by an amount that is statistically significant in the circumstances. (But I do not think that we would *really* accept that if the expected value of the error is zero this constitutes 'correct foresight' irrespective of the variance: that is, no matter how great the variance is.)

It is, on the argument I have been developing, a matter of no possible interest whether a particular belief or expectation is uncertain when compared with some – as it happens, unattainable – ideal state of omniscience. What *is* interesting is whether the belief or expectation is the best that one could arrive at in the circumstances: that is, does it make the best use of such information as is available to the agent concerned? If the best that can be done falls short of some ideal, that may lead to feelings of humility, but it cannot provide reasonable grounds for action or for the revision of actions. By assessing beliefs and expectations in terms of the best use of available information rather than in terms of omniscience, one arrives at a framework of thought that is consistent with fallibilism. One concedes that mere mortals will continue to entertain expectations that will be mistaken in various particular ways; the reasonableness of these agents, however, will manifest itself in their unwillingness to persist in systematic patterns of error, once these have become apparent.

The fundamental mistake that is made in dealing with uncertainty in what we could now call a non-fallibilistic manner, is that it first conflates knowledge with certainty; it then argues, in effect, that since certainty is not attainable, neither is knowledge.[4] That is to say, it is to operate with the tacit presumption that knowledge, to count as such, must be demonstrable, provable, indisputable; which, given the way things are, means that any possibility of knowledge is confined to something like mathematics and formal logic. Philosophically, the position arrived at is known as 'justificationist scepticism'. Thus:

> Justificationism, that is, the identification of knowledge with proven knowledge, was the dominant tradition in rational thought throughout the ages. Scepticism did not deny justificationism: it only claimed that there was (and could be) no proven knowledge and *therefore* no knowledge whatever. For the sceptics 'knowledge' was nothing but animal belief. Thus justificationist scepticism ridiculed objective thought and opened the door to irrationalism, mysticism and superstition. (Lakatos, 1970, p. 94, emphasis in original)

Justificationist sceptics present themselves, however, not in those terms, but simply as sceptics. What we are now in a position to see is that they at the same time both guarantee and trivialise their scepticism by adopting unattainable standards for beliefs to qualify as knowledge. We have seen that Keynes, on occasion, wrote in a way that suggests the adoption of such unattainable standards, although even the most cursory acquaintance with the facts of his life show that he was not reduced to the state of puzzled indecision that a wholehearted adoption of such standards would entail. The contrast between the spirit and the letter of this aspect of Keynes's writing would be made all the more marked by those who attempt to impose on it the consistency of justificationist scepticism.

5. Two schools

In this section, I shall distinguish two contrasting ways in which Keynes's ideas on uncertainty in economic decision-making have been developed by those who have seen them as central to his work. At a later stage, however – in Chapter 6 – all those who have been markedly influenced by this strand in Keynes's work, despite their diversity of response, will reappear as a single interpretative school, the variety of directions taken by its members being united by a common point of departure.

Those commentators on Keynes who have been impressed by his forays into the realm of uncertainty in economic decision-making give, as we have seen, canonical status to his *QJE* article of 1937, in which, in the opening passages, this theme is vigorously expounded. In doing so, however, these commentators may be taken to task for omitting to read the first half of the article in its proper context: namely, the second half. For having completed his brief essay on the incalculability of things in general, Keynes goes on to perform some comparative static exercises on the assumption that consumers' aggregate expenditure is a stable function of consumers' aggregate disposable income and that, furthermore, this stability is maintained in the face of the turbulence arising from the unruly behaviour of private investment and the demand for money. (In the context of Keynes's policy proposals, it is also required that this stability be maintained in the face of arbitrary time paths for fiscal and monetary variables.) All this requires that consumers' expenditure is calculable on the basis of their current disposable incomes and that, therefore, their saving behaviour, by subtraction, is also calculable on the same basis. Accordingly, those who have pointed to this article as an interpretative key owe us, at the very least, an explanation of why, immediately after having provided his key proposition, Keynes engages in analysis in flagrant contradiction with it.

Leaving on one side, however, this purely exegetical issue, we may turn to a consideration of the developments that have been inspired by this theme in Keynes's work. Those who have been influenced by Keynes's forays into the realm of uncertainty and have tried to develop this theme in his work have taken it in one of two ways. First, there are those who have continued to use notions of uncertainty, with its surrounding penumbra of subjectivism, in the same analytically opportunistic way that Keynes himself did. Here I have in mind the group who elect to be called 'post-Keynesian', in the sense of aspiring to go a stage further in what they take to be the direction that Keynes himself was heading. Of paramount importance among those who see themselves as 'post-Keynesian' in this sense is, of course, Joan Robinson. Second, there are those who have tried to follow in a consistent (and, indeed, relentlessly consistent) way the root-and-branch approach to uncertainty that Keynes on occasion adopted. Most notable among these are Shackle (1967, 1972, 1973, 1974) and B. J. Loasby (1976).[5]

The first group – the 'post-Keynesians' – are interested in uncertainty in so far as it helps to show that, under capitalist institutions, the decentralisation of production and investment decisions leads inevitably to chaos and waste. What this group needs to establish, then, is: (1) that the allegedly wayward and unruly nature of production and investment decisions under capitalist institutions is in some way a product of these institutions; and (2) that under some alternative institutional arrangements things would be different (and better).

It is evident, however, that uncertainty and subjectivism in themselves have no bearing on the institution of private property in the means of production, nor on any other institution. The considerations that follow from these ideas are as applicable just as readily to Members of Parliament, Ministers and their officials within the civil service as to entrepreneurs within the private sector of the economy. Indeed, they are just as applicable to the actions of Comrade Prokin of the Reftninsky power station near Sverdlovsk in the Urals when he appears 1,000 miles away in Kharkov in search of truck number 4730092 and the generator that it contains. And, indeed, to his comrades at the Ministry of Railways who were unable to trace its whereabouts; and his further comrade, the director of Reftninsky power station whose plant had been reduced to a standstill by the absence of the missing generator and whose telegrams to his comrades at the Ministry of Railways had proved fruitless (*The Times*, 25 April 1980).

Anyone who has taken even a cursory interest in either the Concorde project, the UK nuclear power programme or the various schemes for a third London airport, will be well aware of the degree of uncertainty that may surround public sector investment projects. Post-Keynesians appear to favour some kind of tripartite institution to oversee investment programmes at the national level, but they do not explain why this will not increase the degree of uncertainty surrounding aggregate investment, rather than reduce it (see for example Eichner, 1979, pp. 176–7, 179–81).

The post-Keynesians are quite happy to make appeals to uncertainty in so far as this enables them to drive a wedge between behaviour and circumstances in some cases; but if the wedge were to become comprehensive, they would be left with no theory at all, all behaviour would appear equally capricious and unintelligible.

The second group has been led to a position that appears to be consistent but analytically nihilistic.[6] A consistent or all-embracing subjectivism is, analytically, a very self-denying thing.[7] If subjectivist logic is followed to the point of becoming convinced that there is nothing for economists to do but to understand certain (praxiological) concepts, then the only problem that remains is that of subjugating one's conscience long enough to draw one's salary in exchange for imparting this piece of wisdom. One could, of course, having got into this state of mind, spend a good deal of time and energy in trying to convince those who engage in macroeconomics, econometric model-building, mathematical economics, general equilibrium theory and so on, of the folly of their ways. But, that task accomplished, there would be nothing left but for the whole profession to shut up shop. This could become a real issue if the current revival of interest in Austrian economics should succumb to the messianic element that is to be found in some of the writings of Austrian subjectivists. We would then be faced with a situation akin to one in which there was an outbreak of Christian Science among the medical profession, or a passion for telekinesis among airline pilots.

6.   Concluding Remarks

This chapter has been concerned with a theme in Keynes's writing that it is convenient but – as we have seen – rather unsatisfactory to refer to as that of uncertainty in economic decision-making. It has been my purpose here to present Keynes's forays into this area as an opportunistic but mild flirtation with subjectivism. I have argued that those who have been impressed and influenced by this strand in Keynes's work fall into two groups:

(1)   those who fail to see that Keynes's encounter with subjectivism is only a passing one;
(2)   those who fail to see that subjectivism, once introduced, cannot be confined within the limits that would suit their analytical purposes.

The former group has no doubt been influenced by Keynes's manner of writing, on occasion, in a way that takes a root-and-branch approach to the matter. I have argued, however, that in taking this root-and-branch approach at all literally they have got hold of the wrong end of the stick. I have also tried to explain the way in which the second group has been led into an unwarrantedly consistent interpretation of Keynes's work. There is probably a moral in all this, although if so it is unlikely to differ very much from those derived in other contexts in which opportunistic flirtation has resulted in misunderstanding among onlookers.

Notes to Chapter 4

1.   In fact, as has been remarked by Joan Robinson (1971, pp. 31–2) this discussion is not at all well focused, and drifts into a discussion of trading on secondary securities markets, in which Keynes points out the difficulty of making short-term capital gains when everybody else is trying to do the same thing.

2.   For example:

On the plane of theory, the revolution lay in the change ... from the principles of rational choice to the problems of decisions based on guesswork and convention. (Robinson, 1973, p. 3.)

Again:

Keynes himself declared in the *Quarterly Journal of Economics* that the *General Theory* was concerned with our mode of coping with, or of concealing from our conscious selves, our ignorance of the future. (Shackle, 1967, p. 6; see also Shackle, 1973, p. 516)

3. The radical implications for the theory of liquidity preference and the determination of *money* prices of Keynes's discussion of uncertainty, and especially of his notion of the resort to *conventional* bases of valuation in the face of changing expectations of future valuations of durable assets, were forcefully and succinctly expressed in Townshend (1937), a paper apparently provoked by Hicks's (1936) review of the *General Theory*, and aimed at challenging what Townshend took to be Hicks's traducing of Keynes's theory of interest. These themes will recur in Chapters 5 and 6.

4. For example: '[Keynes] declares unequivocally that expectations do not rest on anything solid, determinable, demonstrable. "We simply do not know." ' (Shackle, 1973, p. 516)

5. Thus:

If one can summarise in one sentence the theory of employment set forth by Keynes in his article of 1937, it is this: unemployment in a market economy is the result of ignorance too great to be borne. The fully-specified macroeconomic models miss the point – which is precisely that no model of this situation can be fully specified. (Loasby, 1976, p. 167)

Again:

The holder of cash ... in return for giving up his right to the present possession of goods, retains unlimited discretion over the future use of ... resources: he is absolved from giving any indication whatever of the timing or content of his future demands; and there is no automatic provision for meeting his future requirements. The problem is not one of communications, for there is nothing to communicate. (Loasby, 1976, p. 166)

6. For example: 'Keynes's book [*The General Theory*] achieves its triumph by pointing out that the problems it is concerned with are essentially beyond solution.' (Shackle, 1973, p. 516)

7. See, for example, the exchange between Hicks and Lachmann in Rizzo (1979).

5

Hicks's Contribution

---

1. Introduction

The purpose of this chapter is to examine Hicks's contribution
to macroeconomic theory in those respects in which it constitutes
a response to, or a development of, the work of J. M. Keynes.
Thus, while it is narrower in scope than an attempt to assess
Hicks's contribution to macroeconomic theory, it is broader in
scope than an attempt to see Hicks as Keynes's interpreter: for
an interpreter is judged only by the faithfulness with which he
translates the material given to him; he is not required to
extend, recast, criticise or reconstruct that material. We shall
be concerned, then, with what Hicks got out of Keynes's
writings and what he did with it; not with what was 'really'
there. I therefore shall not be concerned with the authenticity or
doctrinal purity of Hicks's Keynesianism.[1]

In considering Hicks's contribution to Keynesian economics,
I shall be concerned with two distinct but related matters. First,
I shall be concerned, in sections 2 and 3, with Hicks's response
to – and in particular his criticisms of – what Keynes himself
actually wrote. However, I shall also, in section 4, be concerned
with Hicks's contribution to those ideas that eventually entered
the public domain as 'Keynesian economics', quite irrespective,
as I noted in Chapter 1, of whether those ideas accurately
reflect what Keynes may or may not have had in mind at some
crucial juncture of his career. I should emphasize that these two
concerns are intended to consist simply of a narrower and a
broader one: they do not involve a contrast between a profound
and intellectually challenging 'Economics of Keynes' on the one
hand, to be set against a vulgar and degenerate 'Keynesian
Economics' on the other. Accordingly, I shall be using the term

'Keynesian' in a robust sense; I use it in full recognition of the possibility of diverse shades of opinion, and of extreme or borderline cases, on the understanding that it is what all these have in common that is important.

These caveats aside, it can be said that over almost the whole range of macroeconomic theory, Hicks was, from the late 1930s onwards, a Keynesian of some variety. The one important exception to this categorisation is on the question of liquidity preference versus loanable funds theories of interest. It is on this one issue that Hicks took a firmly and consistently anti-Keynesian line; and I shall, in what follows, give a good deal of attention to this issue at the expense of such topics as wages and inflation, on which Hicks has pursued what is recognisable as an orthodox Keynesian line. As we shall see, Hicks's Keynesianism was sufficiently whole-hearted for him to be prepared to countenance a degree of analytical laxity in the interests of fostering Keynesian ideas at an early stage of their development. It is of some significance, then, to see the point at which Hicks found he had to dig in his heels and say that Keynes was simply mistaken. Very closely related to this issue is that of Keynes's caricaturing of the 'classical' theory for use as a straw man in his polemical exercises; one's attitude to Keynes as an innovator in economic theory depends quite crucially on whether this caricature is seen as cruel or merely slip-shod. Accordingly, I shall concentrate a good deal of attention on Hicks's conception of 'the classics' vis-à-vis Keynes's treatment of them. The pursuit of this theme will bring us back to the issue, already raised in a general way in Chapter 2, of the analytical procedures corresponding to 'classical' and 'Keynesian' approaches; the concerns here, however, will be more specific than those in the previous discussion, although the framework of ideas already sketched out may be taken as the setting for the account that follows.

As well as attempting to bring into sharp focus Hicks's major criticisms of Keynes's work, it is also my intention to pursue in some detail the development of Hicks's thought, on one aspect of Keynesian economics, from the middle 1930s down to the present. The aspect on which I shall concentrate is that of expectations and the multiplier, for which the line of development leads through Hicks's own work on the trade cycle.

In taking as the starting point for the discussion, as I propose to do, Hicks's review (1936) of Keynes's *General Theory* (1936), we must not lose sight of the work prior to this point, work that gave Hicks such a clear and definite perspective on an obscure and discursive work. Chiefly, of course, Hicks had at his disposal the formidable analytical apparatus that was to emerge somewhat later as *Value and Capital* (1st edn, 1939). He had also made remarkable progress in thinking his way through the foundations of monetary theory, having achieved a firm grip on money in a balance-sheet context and the associated problems of risk in asset-holding decisions.[2] This, then, is the immediate background to our point of departure, 1936.

Hicks reviewed Keynes's *General Theory* when it appeared and, in a way, he has gone on reviewing it throughout his career. His work has been animated directly or indirectly by a determination to *digest* its contents: to bring it into focus and to accommodate its message within some more robust and coherent framework than that which Keynes provided. It can be said that Hicks has attempted to gain first an analytical, later an historical, and finally a practical perspective on the *General Theory*. The first task is that of distilling the analytical core of the *General Theory* as an embodiment of the 'Keynesian system' (this concern becomes central in 'Mr. Keynes and the "Classics" '); the second task is that of providing an embodiment of the 'classical system' such that appropriate comparisons between the two systems can be made (this concern becomes central in 'The "Classics" again'); and the third task is that of reconstructing the analytical core of the *General Theory* in the light of the practical experience gained in the attempts to use this framework as a guide to policy-making (this concern becomes central in *The Crisis in Keynesian Economics* (Hicks 1937; 1967c; 1974).[3]

The object of this inquiry is accordingly to piece together a story part of which ('Mr. Keynes and the "Classics" ') is well known and parts of which have been reconstructed by Hicks himself (1973; 1976, pp. 140–9; 1977, pp. v-xviii). The need to establish the overall outlines of the story is partly a matter of the indisputable importance of Hicks's role in making the *General Theory* accessible to the economics profession at large; but it is also partly a matter of the degree of contention surrounding the exact nature of this role.

Hicks's IS/LM apparatus has provided an analytical receptacle of quite astonishing versatility and resilience within which even the antagonists in protracted controversies have been able to find a common framework for their disputes. As is hardly surprising, however, this apparatus fails to capture the inspirational qualities and the feeling of boundless intellectual possibilities that many found in Keynes's work of the 1930s. Those who responded in this way to Keynes's work saw themselves as participants in an incipient intellectual revolution. But all attempted revolutions – including intellectual ones – depend on the extravagant expectations of the participants; accordingly, all are ultimately disappointing and all lead to a search for scapegoats. Even if, as I believe is true in this case, those involved were misguided in seeing their engagement as a revolutionary one, they still required initially extravagant expectations, and they were still faced with the eventual need for a scapegoat. For these disheartened Keynesian purists, then, Hicks provided an obvious target; and they have not been reluctant to heap on him the responsibility for the setbacks to their early enthusiasms (see, for example, Davidson 1972, p. xi, 1977, p. 277; Minsky 1976, p. 3, 1977, p. 298; Robinson 1971, pp. 82, 88, 98; Weintraub 1977, p. 45). Such treatment has been more conducive to the reinforcement of prejudice than the unravelling of what, as it turns out, is an intriguing episode in intellectual history.

Organizing the discussion of Hicks's criticism and development of Keynes's work in the way I have outlined provides a coverage that is by no means exhaustive. The major casualties of my attempt to present the broad outlines of the story are:

(1) The work in which Hicks (1967) provides a reconciliation of the Keynesian triad of motives for holding money with the textbook triad of functions that it is said to perform, in the course of which he arrives at the suggestive but highly problematic idea that his early programme for monetary theory involved an 'over-voluntarizing' of the transactions demand.[4] (Just how problematic an idea this is should be apparent from the parallels that any attempt to pin it down would have with the attempts, discussed in Chapter 3, to 'de-voluntarize' the phenomenon of unemployment).

(2) The work in which Hicks provides a choice-theoretic formulation of the concept of liquidity and uses this as a

critical tool in discussing Keynes's treatment of and attitude towards 'liquidity preference' (1962; 1967b, pp. 31–7; 1973, p. 11; 1974, pp. 37–57).[5]

(3) Hicks's brief but decisive dismissal of the possibility of reaching stagnationist conclusions with the aid of Keynes's marginal efficiency of capital construction (1936, pp. 248–253).

(4) Hicks's characterization of Keynes's work as a method of approaching problems of economic dynamics in relation to other such methods (1965, pp. 28–35, 76–83, 104–113).

2. Keynes's 'classics' and Hicks's 'classics'

With what is Keynes's theory of employment, interest and money to be contrasted? It would, of course, be fruitless to compare a Keynesian model with a version of the classical system that is simply not addressed to the same questions or problems as the Keynesian model is. A saw is superior to a hammer for the task of cutting wood. But the question of whether saws are, somehow, *generally* superior to hammers is not a very sensible question. The spectacle of someone knocking in a nail with a saw would certainly invite unfavourable comment, comment which assurances about the effectiveness of saws as wood-cutting devices would hardly serve to dismiss; and yet the intellectual equivalent of saw-hammering has been widespread. In other words, translating back from carpentry to economics, if we are to set up 'Keynes versus the classics' as a doctrinal dispute, we must first decide whether Keynes was giving a new answer to the question that the 'classics' (according to his caricature) had been asking, or whether he was really asking a different question.

In all this we are in great danger of becoming enmeshed in a fruitless discussion concerning the label 'classical'; with whether the 'classical' economists constituted, in some sense, a school, whether they did have any recognizable system in common, and whether there ever was a writer who subscribed to 'classical' economics in Keynes's sense. To signal the highly problematic and contentious nature of the term, I have adopted the practice of using it only in quotation marks.

'Mr. Keynes and the "Classics" ' arose out of Hicks's

dissatisfaction with his *Economic Journal* review of the *General Theory* (1973; 1936). The question Hicks addresses in this later paper is the following: In so far as there is, in the *General Theory*, some coherent, systematic analytical scheme or model, what is it? The problem is one of distillation: of rendering down a whole book full of theoretical discussion into some kind of underlying model or framework, from the properties of which the major part of the discussion can be deduced or derived. Thus, the IS/LM model that Hicks provided as the solution to this problem was presented as an interpretation of the 'analytical core' of the *General Theory*. It is evidently not intended to capture everything that is in that book; it quite obviously must disregard the polemical passages and a great deal of discursive and speculative material. The IS/LM framework is offered, accordingly, not as a substitute for the *General Theory*, not as a translation of it into geometry, nor even as a summary of its arguments; rather it is offered, as the opening paragraphs of Hicks's article make plain, as a *guide* to the reader of what, without it, is an exceedingly bewildering and vexatious book. It is in these terms, I would contend, that the IS/LM model should be appraised; for its ability or inability to provide that guidance through the often treacherous territory of Keynes's writing.

The upshot of this paper of Hicks's is that if 'classical' economics is sympathetically understood and properly applied, the conflict between it and Keynesian economics reduces to a matter of analytical procedure or, at most, emphasis. Hicks does try to argue that there are special cases in which the Keynesian approach comes into its own. But if we are prepared to think of these extreme cases as those in which either the IS curve is 'very steep' (almost vertical) or the LM curve is 'very shallow' (almost horizontal), the need to choose between the approaches would not arise, the coverage of the two being identical.

When Hicks looked back on his 'Mr. Keynes and the "Classics"' piece with the benefit of a good deal of hindsight, he came to the conclusion that, although his IS/LM apparatus was a useful one for the exposition of Keynes's central ideas in the *General Theory*, its capacity to serve as a receptacle for 'classical' ideas was more limited. In other words, Hicks's mature reflection was that although he had done justice to Keynes with the IS/LM model, he had been less than fair to the 'classics'. It became apparent that the system that Keynes attacked, and with which he contrasted his own work was not a sympathetic distillation of the best of 'classical' thinking, but a rather stiff, wooden caricature of a 'classical' economist; of a 'classical' economist who animates his ideas in a thoroughly awkward way. If it is true that the more thoughtful and shrewd of the 'classical' writers had been fully alert to 'Keynesian' problems (problems of the influence of monetary conditions on real phenomena) and, indeed, deeply troubled by them, then the discontinuity between 'classical' and 'Keynesian' becomes less abrupt: more a matter of emphasis, focus and analytical procedure than of substance.[6] Bearing all this in mind, I shall now provide a resumé of Hicks's (1967c) argument in 'The "Classics" again'.

The 'classical' approach is to think of the rate of interest as determined by saving and investment ('thrift and productivity'); the Keynesian approach is to think of it as determined by the state of liquidity preference. But consider the effect of an increase in the propensity to save, say. The 'classical' economist would say that this would decrease the rate of interest. But, if he were careful and thorough, he would point out that, with a fixed money supply, this would, as a result of reducing the velocity of circulation ('hoarding'), lead to some downward pressure on output and employment, unless money wages are instantaneously adjusted. The Keynesian economist, on the other hand, would say that the increased propensity to save would (with slower than instantaneously-adjusting money wages) reduce output and employment. But, if he were careful and thorough, he would go on to point out that, with a reduced demand for transactions balances and a fixed supply of money, there would be some downward pressure on the rate of interest. Both the 'classical' and the Keynesian economist would get the same result, provided only that each followed the analysis through rather than abandoning it after the first step. At this level of generality (that is, unless we are in a position to place some restrictions on the parameters of the model) the choice between the 'classical' and the Keynesian approach is merely a matter of procedure. Of course, within Hicks's IS/LM framework, the need to choose one approach rather than the other is not so pressing, for we can simply say that income and the rate of interest are simultaneously determined by *all* the parameters of the system: there is no reason at all why we should want to match up particular endogenous variables with particular sub-sets of parameters.

What Hicks does next is to introduce the assumption of some wages inflexibility (not the assumption that money wages are rigid, but that they are less than perfectly flexible, at any rate in the downward direction) into an otherwise 'classical' approach. What then follows is that there will be a downward-sloping IS curve over the region in which money wages are in some degree inflexible. The reason for this is that if a change in the propensity to save (or to invest) has monetary consequences, then, with a given supply of money, there must be an adjustment either of money wages (and prices) or of interest rates. To the extent that money wages (and prices) are inflexible, some of the burden of adjustment is thrown onto interest rates, and hence the IS curve slopes downwards. Of course, the range over which the system can respond to monetary changes by real (output) adjustments is limited. For simplicity we can think of it as limited at the upper extreme by something that we call 'full employment' (FE); we can similarly think of a lower limit to this region, where, for whatever reason, wages and prices (rather than interest rates) take over the burden of adjustment. (Hicks calls this point 'full unemployment', FU.) Within the FU/FE region, the system behaves in accordance with the IS/LM model, and can be analysed in either the 'classical' or the Keynesian manner, provided the repercussions are properly dealt with. Outside this region, the system behaves in a 'classical' manner: all the burden of adjustment is shouldered by money wages and prices, and the IS/LM apparatus becomes irrelevant.

The next step in Hicks's argument is to point out that the extent of the FU/FE region is really a matter of the time scale we have in mind. If we are thinking of an *immediate* response of money wages and prices, the FU/FE region may be wide; if we are thinking of an *eventual* response, the region will be much smaller. The reconciliation of the two approaches is then within our grasp. The IS/LM model provides an apparatus for short-run problems, while the extreme ('caricatured') 'classical' model provides an apparatus for the analysis of long-run ('full equili-brium') problems. The horizontal IS curve, or the 'classical dichotomy' (of real and monetary phenomena) then becomes a characteristic of long-run equilibrium, having no obvious bearing on short-run resource-utilization and employment problems.

One obvious implication of this is that, if one insists on taking a gladiatorial view of the episode, and seeing it as 'Keynes *versus* the "classics"' (as so many textbooks have done) then one has to be rather careful in one's choice of appropriate contestants, and in one's method for recognizing the winner. If this particular contest is to be fought over the issue of short-run resource-utilization and employment questions, then to pit Keynes against the 'classical' long-period, full equilibrium model is neither appropriate nor illuminating. It guarantees that Keynes wins by a knock-out, but it achieves this only by arranging for his 'classical' adversary to fight with both hands tied behind his back. To make anything like a contest of it, we need to ask what the 'classical' writers had to say about the *same problem to which Keynes was addressing himself*. That is to say, we have to find out not what the 'classical' writers said about things in general, but about short-run resource-utilization and employment problems. Then we can have a contest, if that is the way we want to think.

Leaving 'The "Classics" again', we turn to a paper that was given as a lecture in 1967, and which carries forward the same theme, namely, that the 'classical' writers did have a short-run monetary theory, and that it is with this, rather than their long-run 'full equilibrium' theory that Keynes's *General Theory* should be compared. This paper (Hicks, 1967d), titled 'Monetary theory and history – an attempt at perspective' is aimed at giving some historical depth to the wholly analytical treatment of this theme in 'The "Classics" again'. Hicks does this in various ways: by considerations involving the history of monetary theory; by considerations involving the history of monetary institutions; and by conjectures about the relationship between the two.

Hicks's treatment of the 'classical' short-run theory of money centres on the work of Thornton and J. S. Mill, and its foreshadowing in the writings of Hume. He points out that these writers were perfectly well aware, as is unmistakably clear in Hume, that monetary expansion could have real effects, on output and employment, in the period in which prices are rising to their new level. To the extent that these writers believed in the quantity theory of money and the associated 'classical dichotomy', they did so only in the sense of a (long-run) equilibrium condition, applicable to circumstances in which all the adjustments to a monetary change have taken place. Hicks suggests that at the hands of Ricardo, where the whole focus of attention is on equilibrium states, Hume's insight about the nature of the process of adjustment to monetary change becomes submerged. Hicks had in fact arrived at this point somewhat earlier (in *Capital and Growth* (1965, p. 42)) in connection with his discussion of Adam Smith's approach to the theory of growth.

Hicks's conjecture as to why these 'classical' writers did not place more emphasis on these short-run real consequences of monetary changes is that it was a source of intellectual embarrassment to them; for it led to a conclusion that their instinct told them was wrong, but which they could not dispose of by analytical argument. In Hicks's words:

> They [the 'classical' writers] were terribly afraid that if too much weight were given to short-period effects, it would play into the hands of crude inflationists. The long-period, it would be said, is just a succession of short-periods. Why not keep the stimulus [of monetary expansion] going, when the first dose is exhausted, by another dose? They were afraid of that question, for they did not know the answer to it. Yet they felt in their bones that the suggestion in it was wrong (1967, p. 162).

The instincts that Hicks is here attributing to the 'classical' writers are instincts that display an awareness of both the possibility of monetary changes having real effects, and the dangers of attempting to exploit this possibility. Accordingly, Hicks's 'classics' are inhibited in their policy pronouncements by anxiety, unlike Keynes's 'classics', who are held back by ignorance.

3.   Liquidity preference and loanable funds

In discussing the relationship between the work of Keynes and of Hicks, there is a third individual who must make an appearance sooner or later. That individual is Sir Dennis

Robertson. There are at least two reasons why he should be brought into the picture. First, of those who were critical of the monetary theory of Keynes's *General Theory*, Robertson's (1940) critique was perhaps the most penetrating and certainly the most lucid.[7] Second, the analytical basis of Robertson's critical response to Keynes's theory of money and interest is practically identical with the analytical basis of Hicks's sympathetic response. Thus, we have the intriguing state of affairs, as regards the monetary and interest theory of the *General Theory*, that Hicks and Robertson agreed with one another as far as any purely *analytical* questions were concerned, and yet disagreed quite fundamentally in their overall assessment of the merit of the theoretical developments involved.

We shall consider next the analytical issues, first as presented by Hicks, and then as presented by Robertson. It will emerge that Hicks and Robertson agreed that Keynes's liquidity preference theory of interest differs from the 'classical' loanable funds approach not by virtue of its *substance*, but only as a matter of analytical procedure. In all this we adopt the usual convention that there is a plane of discourse on which it makes sense to talk of 'the' rate of interest.

Hicks expounded the equivalence of liquidity preference and loanable funds approaches to the theory of interest in a very clear but necessarily condensed form in the *Economic Journal* review of 1936; this interpretation was present, although peripherally, in 'Mr. Keynes and the "Classics" ' (1937). The fullest expression, by Hicks, of this interpretation, is to be found in Chapter XII of *Value and Capital* (1946, pp. 153–162). Here Hicks adopts a general equilibrium framework, and shows that it can make no difference of substance which price is associated, in the model, with which market (including among our list of 'markets' one for the holding of money). Once it is admitted that each trader faces a budget constraint[8] it must be conceded that not all markets are independent of one another. Thus, once we have embarked on *general* equilibrium theory, it makes very little sense to speak, for example, of 'the price of widgets being determined in the market for widgets'. Rather, in so far as one can give any causal interpretation of a general equilibrium model (and the more fastidious practitioners of the art would avoid doing so) it would be that the vector of relative prices is determined by the whole configuration of parameters (this is precisely what the reduced-form equations tell us, reading them 'from right to left'). Thus, whether we eliminate the money equation (as in the 'classical' approach) or the borrowing and lending ('loanable funds') equation (as in the Keynesian approach) is entirely a matter of analytical procedure: that is, it is at most a matter of convenience. All this would appear platitudinous to a general equilibrium theorist, but to someone trained in the Marshallian tradition of partial equilibrium analysis it goes against the grain. The disposition dies hard to think of each price as determined in the market in which the good in question is traded. Accordingly, controversy about whether the rate of interest is determined in the market for 'loanable funds' (by borrowing and lending) or in the money market (by 'liquidity preference') was rife in the late 1930s and beyond, despite the existence of a well-articulated framework in which the controversy could be shown to depend on a false dichotomy: to involve the setting up of a misguided opposition of views which can be very readily reconciled with one another. But, before *Value and Capital*, how much interest was there in England (outside the London School of Economics) in the work of Walras? To the extent that British economists of this period were either unaware of, or uninterested in, the economic theory of Walras, we may attribute some of the pointlessness and inconclusiveness of this controversy to a state of intellectual insularity.

A reservation should be noted concerning the discussion so far. It is that we have been concerned with the equivalence of 'classical' and Keynesian theories of the rate of interest within the confines of equilibrium analysis. It is another question whether the equivalence still holds if we widen our horizon to include the possibility of disequilibrium states. It has been argued by some that the equivalence cannot be sustained in the wider context, and that indeed, where the two theories diverge, it is the liquidity preference theory that gives the 'wrong' results regarding interest rate movements (Patinkin 1958; Johnson 1961). But this has been disputed by Tsiang (1966, pp. 340–1), who has argued that, if the analysis is followed through properly, the equivalence holds under both equilibrium and disequilibrium states. But the Tsiang argument depends on the insistence that the 'net acquisition of cash through trading' is not the same thing as the 'demand for money', a distinction which, in the terms I have been using in Chapter 3, amounts to a 'de-voluntarising' of the holding of money balances.

Leaving Hicks for the moment, we turn to Robertson's treatment of the same issue. Robertson (1940) set out his criticisms of Keynes's *General Theory* doctrines on the rate of interest in a series of lectures given at the London School of Economics in 1939. His objections to the claim that Keynes's liquidity preference theory of interest is either novel, or in substantive conflict with the 'classical' loanable funds approach, are made very clear (Robertson, 1940, pp. 1–28). The point, as it turns out, is a purely logical one: that whatever something *is*, there are many things that it is not; and it hardly makes much sense to say, of the various things that it is not, that one of them rather than another is what it *really* isn't. Yet this is what Keynes was claiming: that there can be such priorities.

The individual trader may dispose of his money income by allocating it between the following three exhaustive and mutually exclusive categories:

(1)   spending (on commodities);
(2)   net lending, i.e. buying bonds;
(3)   hoarding, i.e. additions to money holding.

In the light of this classification, let us turn to the controversy over the determination of interest rates.

The 'classical' idea was that interest is the reward for *not-spending*, i.e. it is the inducement to refrain from spending. In apparent contrast, the Keynesian doctrine is that interest is the reward for *not hoarding*, i.e. it is the inducement to part with liquidity.[9]

The resolution of this apparent conflict between the 'classical' and the Keynesian doctrine now emerges. In terms of our categories for the disposal of income, the resolution is that lending is, at one and the same time, both not-spending *and* not-hoarding, in just the same way that being Keynes is, at one and the same time, to be both not-Hayek and not-Beveridge; and in just the same way that arguing whether Keynes is really not-Hayek rather than not-Beveridge is a pointless exercise: one can hardly establish priorities among what someone (or something) is not.

Keynes never conceded the force of this objection, nor did he ever explain why he thought it misguided or beside the point. He obviously had no patience with this particular line of argument, and opposed it by dismissive counter-assertion. When Harrod suggested that the liquidity preference theory of interest might need some qualification, Keynes wrote back complaining that Harrod had not understood him; just as, later, in correspondence with Ohlin, he was to denounce the loanable funds theory as a 'fundamental heresy' while omitting to explain what was wrong with it; and, in an article, he simply reiterated that this theory and his own liquidity preference theory were 'radically opposed' without explaining how their implications differed (1973, pp. 544–52, 185, 202). Well, Keynes was a forceful personality and he was used to getting his own way in arguments. Of course, one can see what he was driving at. In so far as resources are scarce, one needs an inducement for people to refrain from consumption in order to free resources for investment. But if there are unemployed resources anyway, there is no longer the need for consumption to be reduced in order to release resources for investment: there exists the possibility of mobilizing the unemployed resources without any current consumption being foregone. So much is unexceptionable at the level of abstract possibilities. But the question then arises: can one, in a market system, absorb unemployed resources in expanded investment, quite independently of, and without having any effect on, interest rates? As we have seen, Hicks's painstaking analysis shows that the answer is 'no': only in the extreme case of a perfectly horizontal LM curve do we have a monetary sector in which the interest rate is determined independently of real forces. (As we have seen in Chapter 2, however, this case may have far greater relevance to the formulation and conduct of macroeconomic policies than would be apparent from its analytical restrictiveness.)

Although there was some sense in Keynes's instinct about the functioning of interest rates in a depression, his attempt to translate this instinct into a model, a piece of analysis, is flawed. But Keynes evidently had unshakable confidence in his own instinct, and continued to defend (what he took to be) his analytical expression of it. So began a protracted debate on 'liquidity preference versus loanable funds', which Patinkin (1976, p. 140) has rightly described as 'pointless and depressing'.

It is not a matter of this criticism from Robertson coming too late: of the book being in print and Keynes having to stand by what he had written. In fact Robertson had made the point that the rate of interest is determined jointly by the influence of the propensity to save and the productivity of capital, as well as by liquidity preference, when he had been sent the proofs of the *General Theory* in February 1935. Evidently, however, Keynes was not prepared to countenance such doubts (1973, pp. 512–20).

There is no doubt that, at almost all intellectual and practical levels, Keynes's instinct won the day against Robertson's analysis. It is a considerable tribute to Keynes's powers of persuasion that, having got himself into a muddle, he could induce the major part of the profession to share it with him. Accordingly, the liquidity preference theory of interest duly became enshrined in a crop of textbooks, presented as being both a *new* theory and a theory in substantive *conflict* with the 'classical' loanable funds theory.

Although Robertson was, as we can now see, correct, where Keynes was wrong, his criticisms were not well taken. Even Hicks, who, as we have seen, agreed analytically with Robertson's line of argument, eventually came to see them as rather carping. He wrote (Hicks, 1942, p. 54):

> For my own part, I rather regret the amount of criticism contained in these essays [Robertson's *Essays in Monetary Theory*, 1940] – particularly in that printed at the beginning of the book, the London lectures of 1939 ['Mr. Keynes and the Rate of Interest']. Of all great economists, Mr. Keynes is probably the most Impressionist; the *General Theory*, in particular, needs to be read at a distance, not worrying too much about detail, but looking principally at the general effect. At least, that is how I have read it myself, and it seems that as a result I retain a higher opinion of it than Professor Robertson does. His own criticisms sometimes remind one of a man examining a Seurat with a microscope and denouncing the ugly shapes of the individual dots. It is very probable that the Impressionist method is not particularly appropriate to the higher economics (though it may be suitable enough for more popular writing); however, it is Mr. Keynes's method, and in his hands it has some countervailing virtues.

It is evident that Hicks is here advocating that Keynes's work
– and particularly his theory of interest rates – be read in a
charitable spirit. But his metaphor of Impressionism and Seurat,
although vivid and suggestive is not really convincing. Clearly,
just as one should see a painting as a whole, rather than
examining the appearance of its elements, so one should read
abstract theory and analysis with an eye on the overall tendency
or upshot. But although a metaphor may suggest an argument,
it does not itself constitute one. What is supposed to correspond,
in Keynes's work, to the shape of the individual dots in the
Seurat, or to the judgement that they are ugly? Is it being
suggested that, just as one can create a pleasing painting from
elements which may be individually unattractive, so one can
expound a correct doctrine out of analytical exercises which are
individually mistaken (or confused)? If this is the suggestion, it
really needs to be argued; and it does seem to be advocating a
degree of charity that one would not generally advocate, and
that, if it were advocated as a general rule would amount to the
abandonment of the idea that economics is an academic,
intellectual activity which can make progress through a process
of criticisms and rational discourse. It seems to be suggested
that in the case of Keynes we should assess his conclusions
independently of the weight and soundness of the arguments he
uses to arrive at them: it amounts to the proposal to treat
Keynes as *authoritative*.

One way of interpreting Hicks's position is to say that he was
comparing the performance of the 'classical' approach with
(what he took to be) the *potential* of Keynes's approach.[10] This
is, of course, a dangerous comparison to make, for there is far
more scope for enthusiasm in forming one's estimate of Keynesian potential than there is in perceiving 'classical' performance. Indeed, intellectual innovation and progress demand that
we are prepared on some occasions to permit such dangerous
comparisons, in which our conjecture about the potential of an
undeveloped research programme is compared with the much
firmer knowledge of the performance of existing approaches.
But, equally, the fact that scholarship should not degenerate
into mere matters of faith or fashion requires that there be some
limit on how long we treat a research programme as 'promising':
there must come a time when we are prepared to judge the new
approach in terms of its performance. To require that a

particular approach be given the permanent benefit of the doubt is to require that others should share not only one's own conjectures about future intellectual developments, but also that they share one's current enthusiasms. It is, in short, to convert research into proselytizing.

The reason all this has a bearing on Hicks is that Hicks found himself with a foot in each camp. On purely intellectual grounds, he was with Robertson; on the wider view, he was with Keynes. The only question that remains is whether he would see the debate in purely intellectual terms, or, as we might say, pragmatically, in the light of existing circumstances. It can't have been an easy or pleasant dilemma to live with.

Robertson's criticisms of Keynes's theory of money and interest were not confined to Keynes's claim that the liquidity preference and loanable funds approaches were 'radically opposed'. He also advanced the argument that 'liquidity preference' (in relation to the money supply), far from determining the rate of interest, actually leaves its determination dangling in mid-air. This criticism focuses on Keynes's well-known theory of the speculative demand for money. In this, considerations of expected capital gains and losses resulting from fluctuations of the interest rate about some normal rate (about which estimates will differ between speculators) provide a rationale for the holding of money balances (rather than bonds) to an extent depending on the expected movement of interest rates, and therefore on the level of interest rates relative to the level that is believed to be normal. All this is now standard textbook fodder. Speculators adjust their portfolios in order to make capital gains or avoid capital losses, and they do this by making substitutions between money and bonds in the light of their expectations. Even leaving aside the 'transactions demand' for money, as being a further consideration that must be introduced before we can say anything definite, can this be an adequate account of the elements involved in the determination of the rate of interest? Robertson's answer (1940, p. 25) is 'no':

Mr. Plumtre of Toronto, in an unpublished paper, has aptly compared the position of lenders of money under this theory [Keynes's theory of the speculative demand for money] with that of an insurance company which charges its clients a premium, the only risk against which it insures them being the risk that its premium will be raised. If we ask what ultimately governs the judgements of wealth-owners as to why the rate of interest should be different in the future from what it is today, we are surely led straight back to the fundamental phenomena of Productivity and Thrift.

It had long been known that the market rate of interest (which, of course, is a money rate) can diverge from the 'underlying, real rate' – the rate that would have obtained in the absence of monetary disturbance, if the monetary system worked so as to reveal rather than disguise the real forces. (Indeed this is central to the teaching of Wicksell.) The monetary disturbance can come from the workings of the banking system, from the policy of the central bank, or from the behaviour of speculators. Keynes introduces, and indeed focuses on, such monetary disturbances in the determination of interest rates. What he does not tell us is what it is that is being disturbed: what the monetary disturbance is a disturbance *of*.

Keynes's theory of the speculative demand for money must therefore be seen as an essay in the economics of pure chaos. The speculators speculate, but what are they really speculating *on*? The answer Keynes gives is the behaviour of other speculators. Of course, when it comes to the *practice* of speculation Keynes must be admitted to be something of an authority. When one plays the market on the basis of day-to-day trading with a view to capital gains (rather than income), then one clearly does not spend much time pondering on the forces of productivity and thrift that lie behind the general *level* of interest rates (and the return on other assets) about which day-to-day fluctuations take place. When one boils a pan of soup, the surface bubbles; but in order to have bubbles one has to have a surface, and, for this, one has to have soup. It is true that the bubbles are *on* the surface, but what is it that keeps them up there? The answer cannot confine itself to the process of boiling or of bubbling; it must pay attention to the amount of soup in the pan. To one who has learnt to float among the bubbles this may not be at all apparent. He may even be led to the view, firmly based on first-hand experience, that soup is really nothing but bubbles; and that bubbles, in their turn, are entirely a matter of boiling (a dynamic process), not of such static, timeless, unhistorical things as the quantity of soup and the base area of the pan. Indeed, if the issue were not so vividly concrete, there could develop a controversy between the 'boiling and bubbling' school on the one hand, and the exponents of the 'area and volume' approach on the other. The view that a boiling and bubbling approach could be concerned with just another aspect of what was being considered by the area and volume approach would not sound very plausible. Volumes and areas can neither boil nor bubble. The exponents of the boiling and bubbling school would naturally insist that the two theories are radically opposed.

4.   Expectations and the multiplier process

In the Keynesian system, the multiplier serves as the link between changes in investment expenditure and changes in real income and output: it is the process by means of which changes in expenditure become pervasive and come to have pervasive influence. The question that immediately suggests itself, however, and which Keynes himself did not tackle, is that of the circumstances under which the multiplier will operate at all reliably. It is obvious, of course, that in order for a general expansion of output to be possible, there must be spare capacity; it is also well known that the existence of a reliable connection between investment changes and income changes depends, at least, on there being a stable consumption function (this component of the multiplier process has accordingly been closely scrutinized). But that is by no means all there is to it. For there remain the questions of why and how the various changes in expenditure are supposed to be translated into changes in real output. Thus:

(1)   Why should the change in investment expenditure appear as a change in real investment rather than as an increase in the price of capital goods and the rate of interest? Why does it not result in a reduction in expenditure (and thence investment) elsewhere in the economy?

(2)   Why should producers, when they experience increased sales resulting from the additional expenditure, respond by increasing output and employment rather than by allowing inventories to fall or by raising prices?

The questions concerning the extent of price level changes associated with the multiplier process are by-passed in Keynes by the device of working in real terms (or, in Keynes's own version, in 'wage units'). In this respect, Hicks has largely followed suit, except for his attempts, latterly, to introduce a distinction between 'fix-price' and 'flex-price' markets so that the multiplier theory would apply strictly if all markets were of the 'fix-price' type (1974, pp. 23–30).[11] But the remaining questions, concerning the manner in which production may respond to expenditure changes that are presumed to be real (and persistent), is indeed tackled by Hicks (1974, pp. 9–30). In this way he may be thought of as putting forward the elements for a theory of expenditure-induced macro movements in which crowding out and, to some extent, price-level movements, appear, along with the multiplier process, as possibilities. As we shall see, in unravelling the processes in which the operation of the multiplier are embedded, the treatment of producers' expectations – how we suppose that they are formed and revised and, in particular, how we can render their treatment analytically manageable – is crucial. As we shall also see, if the lines of development initiated by Hicks are pursued, one is confronted by the need for a more explicit and detailed formulation of the theory of the adjustment of expectations by producers, a need that leaves the theory of the multiplier looking far more like a black box of the kind that is said to preclude access to the precise workings of the monetarist model.

Hicks first turned his attention to the operation of the multiplier in his original *Economic Journal* review (1936) of the *General Theory*. There he raises the general question of the circumstances regarding supply elasticities that are required for the operation of the multiplier. In particular, he draws attention to the role of stocks of various kinds in sustaining the multiplier process while the initiating expansion of investment expenditure is being translated into increases in output and employment.

In his recent revision of the theory of the multiplier, Hicks (1974, pp. 11–23) again lays great stress on the role of inventories in sustaining the multiplier process. His focus is on what we might call the 'breathing space effect'. Hicks's reasoning is as follows. Between an increase in investment expenditure and the associated increase in production, there will be a time-lag. During this time-lag, expenditure will have increased but production is still unchanged, so that over this period (unless we happen to be in a phase of rapid planned stockbuilding) inventories will be falling. As production levels are finally increased, the locus of falling inventories is transmitted backwards through the whole network of production, finally reaching stocks of raw materials. Now, provided this expansionary impulse succeeds in getting itself transmitted through the whole network of production, economic activity can reconstitute itself at a higher level, consistent with the increased expenditure. But suppose, at some stage in the network of production, inventories are depleted before revised output decisions can be implemented. This means that there is a shortage, or bottleneck, for those producers who use this output as an input. In such circumstances, prices may be forced to play their allocative role (or some other method of rationing may induce a process of reallocation). It is at this point that there must be a breakdown of any idea of a uniform or overall or pervasive increase in the intensity with which existing resources are utilized. For the obstacle to the expansionary process is a problem of relative scarcities, in which the resources that are required to sustain the expansion have to be released from alternative uses.

According to Hicks's account, then, the conditions favourable to an expenditure-induced expansion are that inventories are relatively high in order to sustain the expansion during the lag between changes in sales and changes in production. (In fact, this analysis can be translated, as Hicks does, from fix-price into flex-price terms; in the latter case, the circumstances conducive to fiscal leverage are that the prices of the relevant goods are low compared to some 'normal' level of prices, so that stocks will be released as prices rise in response to the production increase.) But Hicks does not go on to ask the questions: why should inventories in general be abnormally high?

Such a question brings us inescapably to the role of expectations in the multiplier process. Again, this is an issue that Hicks first raised in his original review (1936, pp. 242–3) of the *General Theory*. In that review, Hicks makes the point that in Keynes's method of analysis, long-term expectations are to be regarded as part of the *data* of the problem. The analytical problem then, Hicks makes clear, is to find an equilibrium relative to a particular set of (given, long-term) expectations. As regards the determination of this short-period equilibrium, however, it is taken for granted by Keynes that short-term expectations (regarding current sales) are always fulfilled. Thus, when expenditure changes, short-term expectations underlying production and employment decisions are (correctly) revised, but long-term expectations underlying investment decisions are unaffected and, in Keynes's system, stubbornly pessimistic. This seems straightforward enough. But to distill this from the *General Theory* is a considerable feat, for the *General Theory* is a somewhat opaque piece of work. Here Hicks had the considerable advantage of being able to appreciate Keynes's method in the light of the method he was himself developing in the course of working on *Value and Capital*, that is, the method of temporary equilibrium. Hicks would be able to discern that what Keynes had hit on was not itself the method of temporary equilibrium (it was not nearly well-defined and systematic enough to constitute that); but on the other hand it had much in common with this method, in particular its device of considering an equilibrium relative to expectations extending beyond the considered time-period, expectations which, from the point of view of that time-period, must be treated as 'data'. It is evident that such a method has great attractions – it appears analytically very powerful in its ability to disentangle (or even to define) specifically short-run problems. Of course, this can be achieved only at the expense of the shockingly artificial separation of expectations into a short-run component (which is always fulfilled within the current short-period), and a long-run component (which is given, and completely impervious to what goes on within the current period). Of course, such a method cannot be justified (or not directly justified) on any kind of empirical grounds. Its only possible justification is on grounds of analytical convenience: it enables us to proceed with theorizing that can be made manageable, and has some chance of reaching definite conclusions. The only legitimate defence of using such a dangerous method would be to claim a full appreciation of its limitations and a constant awareness that, in practice, short-run problems do not appear neatly packaged and guaranteed independent of the longer-run considerations arising from the economic processes in which they are embedded, and from which they have been abstracted by analytical fiat.

As it happens, Hicks was himself to make extensive use of the multiplier, some years later, as a component of his *Contribution to the Theory of the Trade Cycle*, in which he put forward an ingenious cycle-generating mechanism involving a basically explosive cumulative movement constrained to oscillate by floors and ceilings (1950, pp. 95–107). In looking at this monograph from the point of view of the use and development of the multiplier theory, we should not lose sight of the task to which the theorizing is directed, the skill with which this task is achieved, and the need, in making this possible, to brush aside a number of complications to the postulated cyclical mechanism.

One such complication that is recognized, discussed, but finally avoided is the role of inventories in the cycle (1950, pp. 38–9, 47–55). It is avoided by the device of choosing the time period of analysis to be the length of time (assumed constant) that it takes for output to be increased sufficiently to offset the rate of inventory decumulation resulting from an initiating rise in expenditure: the increase in *realized* net investment accordingly appears always one period later than an increase in *planned* net investment (1950, pp. 53–4). This leaves working capital as a spear-carrier in a drama having fixed capital in the leading role.

When we come to the treatment of expectations, however, it becomes necessary to read between the lines of Hicks's monograph. What we find between the lines is that, in the multiplier/ accelerator model adopted, production decisions (proximately governed by the multiplier) are always based on correct expectations about current sales; investment decisions (proximately governed by the acceleration principle) are always based on mistaken expectations about the trend in sales, the mistakes arising from producers' naïve extrapolation of cyclical movements in order to determine the requirement for *fixed* capital. The mechanism of the model accordingly involves producers in constantly mistaking cyclical changes in sales for secular ones; never learning that this is what they are doing; but perfectly anticipating the cyclical changes that are being persistently misinterpreted. The producers in such a world display a curious conjunction of short-run intelligence and long-run stupidity, a conjunction that is not exposed to view, the treatment of expectation in this monograph being left out of focus. This lack of explicitness is made evident by the fact that Hicks felt it necessary to emphasize, in the Preface to the third impression of the book that: '... the inducement of investment, as I conceive it, and as it is described in Chapter 4, is not a mere matter of technical necessity; it works through the state of mind of entrepreneurs, having a close connection with what I have called in another place the "elasticity of expectations" ' (1956, p. vi). But the rather cavalier treatment of expectations in the trade cycle monograph cannot be seen as a mere oversight, as this postscript might suggest; rather it is absolutely necessary to get results from the multiplier and accelerator used in combination. It leads to the most glaring deficiency of the multiplier/ accelerator model, namely that it generates a cycle which, no matter how regular it is nor how often repeated, remains a source of continual surprise to transactors; they never learn that booms give way to recessions, nor that recessions are superseded by recoveries.

In *Value and Capital*, Hicks (1946, p. 296) had touched on this matter in the following way:

Among such other causes [of the ending of a boom] we may have to include a mere sense on the part of business men that the boom has gone on about as long as booms do usually go on; so that the mere lapse of time shifts their expectations downwards. Even in a very cycle-conscious world it is hard to attach much importance to this.

But the difficulties of attaching importance to such considerations are not explained, so the remark remains enigmatic.

We may conclude that the main source of instability making for cumulative movements in the multiplier/accelerator model is the irrational expectations that are built into the acceleration principle as a theory of investment in *fixed* capital. Now, the irrationality of long-run expectations was something vigorously propounded by Keynes in the *General Theory*, and constitutes his ground for seeing investment in fixed capital as the volatile, destabilizing element in the economy. All this has been discussed in detail in the previous chapter, and need not be repeated here. In the context of the present discussion, however, it is appropriate to add an acknowledgement of the fact that Hicks came to reconsider this aspect of the *General Theory* some twenty years after completing his work on the theory of the trade cycle. On this later occasion, he writes (1969, p. 313):

When I reviewed the *General Theory*, the explicit introduction of expectations was one of the things which I praised; but I have since come to feel that what Keynes gave with one hand, he took away with the other. Expectations do appear in the *General Theory*, but (in the main) they appear as *data*; as autonomous influences that come in from outside, not as elements that are moulded in the course of the process that is being analyzed. Perhaps it is that famous (but I now think rather wicked) chapter on 'Long-term expectations' which is the root of the trouble. For one can grant that there exists an irrational element in expectations (the element of which Keynes made so much) without conceding that they are so irrational as to be random – and therefore incapable of being moulded, at least to some extent, by policy.

In seeing Keynes's Chapter 12 as basically mischievous and, from the would-be theorist's point of view, nihilistic, Hicks puts himself in sharp contrast with that group of Keynesian interpreters who have seen Chapter 12 as the highlight of the *General Theory*: an interpretative key to the remainder of that work and perhaps even its central message.[12] These interpreters have been greatly impressed by the destructive consequences that Keynes's Chapter 12 has for the 'classical' system that he was attacking; what they fail to recognize is that the type of considerations to be found in Chapter 12 would have just as destructive consequences, if they were turned in that direction, for Keynes's own positive contribution to economic analysis. In fact, the ostensibly destructive facets of the *General Theory* can be reconciled with its constructive parts only if we are prepared to look at them in terms of the *tactics of persuasion*, rather than in terms of abstract propositions and their logical relations. One can make most sense out of the *General Theory* by regarding the destructive parts as being concerned with clearing the grounds to make room for the constructive parts.

I would therefore argue that Hicks's is a sounder interpretation of the *General Theory* than that of those who take Chapter 12 at its face value. It appears that one can make far more sense of Keynes's position as a whole by treating Chapter 12 as a manifestation of animal spirits rather than as a carefully considered piece of analysis.

5.   Concluding remarks

In coming to an assessment of Hicks's contribution to Keynesian economics, we have to distinguish between his commentaries on Keynes's own writing (where I have focused on the points of clear disagreement) and his work on the development of what can be broadly considered as 'Keynesian' ideas, in which sphere I have focused on one particular theme. Putting the two spheres together, we see Hicks as both one of the most severe critics of Keynes's own analysis *and* as one of the most vigorous and persistent of those who have tried to refine and strengthen the basic ideas that emerged from the controversy instigated by Keynes. The contrast is an instructive one, for it shows that Hicks's commitment to Keynesianism manifests itself despite a clear awareness on his part of the analytical shortcomings of the particular form it had then been given. All this is at its clearest in Hicks's disagreement with Robertson over the theory of interest, for in that case the two were in complete agreement on all relevant analytical matters. The disagreement concerned Hicks's belief that, despite all the admitted analytical shortcomings of the *General Theory*, Keynes was on to something: that the important thing was not what he had succeeded in saying, but what he was trying to say. In sensing that Keynes was on to something, Hicks must have been very much conditioned by the feeling that the something seemed in many respects to be very like what he was on to himself; but how much of his own well-developed insights was he reading into Keynes's work?

Within the first sphere of the interpretation and criticism of Keynes's *General Theory*, we have seen that the tasks that Hicks set himself were partly expository – restating Keynes's ideas with an increased degree of analytical discipline – and partly a matter of adjudicating Keynes's claims, the analytical restatement being such as to make this possible. His verdict is that Keynes was misguided in presenting his own theory as an attack on and as in conflict with the 'classical' system. The 'classical' system that Keynes set up as a target for attack was simply addressed to different sorts of problems from those he was concerned with and, worse still, ignored those aspects of the writings of the 'classics' that were concerned with precisely his sort of problems. Keynes's method of associating, on the one hand, national income determination with saving and investment decisions and, on the other hand, interest rate determination with asset-holding decisions (as between money and bonds), is demonstrated by Hicks to be not a new theory but rather an alternative analytical procedure which, properly handled, leads to the same results as the previously-adopted procedure. This all seems very hard on Keynes; and so it is. Yet one cannot begin to appreciate the development of Hicks's thought on the basis of this analytical verdict alone. For despite his analytical verdict's being so uncompromisingly harsh, Hicks's attitude to the *General Theory* was (after some early wavering) unambiguously favourable: indeed he regarded himself as a convert to Keynes's way of thinking (see, for example, 1974, p.5).

Within the wider sphere of Hicks's continuing development of Keynesian ideas, we have seen how his early awareness of the multifarious difficulties surrounding the multiplier construct was supplanted by a willingness to make use of this construct as a component of a postulated cycle-generating mechanism, and, more recently, by a renewed interest in the difficulties he had originally discerned in its operation. It has become apparent that Hicks has repeatedly set himself the task of thinking about the multiplier as an unfolding process, in which it is necessary to understand how changed levels of expenditure impinge on, and modify, the expectations and hence the plans of producers. In this way he is effectively asking the key question for Keynesians: under what circumstances will fiscal policy have a reliable effect on the level of economic activity, and precisely what is the mechanism by which its effects reach decisions on output and employment?

Notes to Chapter 5

1. Professor Coddington left a note to this section which he was not able to develop fully before his tragic death. It reads:

    Make it clear that I don't think Hicks is the only one involved in developing Keynesian Economics (mention Hansen, Samuelson, Modigliani, Meade, Harrod, Tobin, etc ... as well as those – e.g. Joan Robinson – to be explicitly discussed in the book).
    (Could even mention such as Lange, Lerner, Harris (Seymour), Leontief, etc.?)

2. For a retrospective account by Hicks of this episode in his intellectual development, see Hicks, 1973, pp. 4–7.

3. I shall be concerned here with certain aspects only of this latter work. For a more thorough appraisal of it see Fisher, 1976.

4. This work of Hicks has been the object of severe criticism on analytical grounds, see Harris, 1969; Perlman, 1971. Hicks, however, has subsequently reaffirmed his position without acknowledgement of the criticisms (1977, p. xiv).

5. For a judicious appraisal of this line of thought see Fisher (1976, pp. 308–11).

6. Keynes himself was evidently persuaded of the revolutionary nature of his own work, as his much-quoted letter to G. B. Shaw of 1 January 1935 makes clear (1973, pp. 492–3).

7. Further criticisms of Keynes's interest rate doctrine in the *General Theory* was advanced by, amongst others, Ohlin (1937); this led to a fruitless exchange in the pages of the *Economic Journal*, in which Keynes (1973, pp. 183–223) showed himself unable to distinguish between a loanable funds theory of interest on the one hand, and a saving and investment theory on the other.

8. Tsiang has pointed out that what is usually referred to in this context as a 'budget constraint' or an 'income constraint' has in fact got nothing to do with either budgeting or income (1966, p. 331). Rather it expresses the supposition that goods are acquired only through acts of trading in which equal values are exchanged. Accordingly, Tsiang suggests, this condition should properly be called a 'fair exchange constraint'.

9. Thus, in Keynes's own words, we read: 'The habit of overlooking the relation of the rate of interest to hoarding may be a part of the explanation why interest has been usually regarded as the reward of not-spending, whereas in fact it is the reward of not-hoarding' (1936, p. 174); see also (1936, pp. 166–8) and, for the faithful reproduction of this attitude see, for example, Dillard (1958, p. 162–4).

10. Those whom, in Chapter 6, I shall designate 'fundamentalist Keynesians', continued to make the comparison between (neo-) 'classical' performance and Keynesian potential even after the Keynesian approach had had several decades in which to realize its potential. Their writings on the theory of money and interest tend therefore to be essentially programmatic: their writing concerns advocacy of a particular programme of research, accompanied by the assurance that this line is indeed a promising one. Thus Joan Robinson could write, in 1973, that 'The Keynesian revolution still remains to be made both in teaching economic theory and in forming economic policy' (1973, p. 11). Similarly, J. A. Kregel could write, in the same year: 'To ask for an alternative to the neoclassical theory comparable in precision and beauty is naïve. But the *potential* for a truly alternative ['post-Keynesian'] approach exists, the problem is to expose and explain this potential . . .' (Kregel, 1973, p. xvii, emphasis added).

11. There are, however, serious obscurities involved in Hicks's use of the fix-price concept, as Fisher (1976, pp. 306–7) has pointed out.

12. See, for example, Davidson (1972, pp. 10–32); Minsky (1976, pp. 55–68); Robinson (1973, pp. 3–6); Shackle (1974, pp. 67–83). This is a sample from the group I shall later designate as 'fundamentalist Keynesians'. Members of this group have characteristically taken Chapter 12 of the *General Theory* in conjunction with Chapter 17 on 'The essential properties of interest and money', so arriving at a concern with the possibility of macroeconomic instability arising from changes in the private sector's willingness to hold its wealth in more or less liquid forms.

6

The Search for First Principles

1. Introduction

In *The General Theory of Employment, Interest and Money* and elsewhere, Keynes (1936,1937) attacked a body of theory that he designated 'classical'. We have seen in the previous chapter that there are serious problems concerning Keynes's conception of what he was attacking, and whether, indeed, the object of his engagement should in fact have been cast in such an adversary role. But quite apart from these issues of the appropriateness of Keynes's debating tactics, there is no doubt that his work was recognised as posing a threat to some quite deeply entrenched aspects of the methods of economic analysis practised at the time. The purpose of this chapter is to inquire into the various ways in which methods of economic analysis have come to terms with this threat, either by responding to it or by reinforcing it with further threats. It seeks to ask the question: 'What has to be changed or sacrificed in order to accommodate Keynesian ideas within standard methods of analysis?' Its theme will be the variety of ways in which this may be done, of which variety three broad types will be presented and the contrasts between them explored.

The first task is accordingly to characterise the method of analysis of that body of theory in opposition to which Keynes presented his own. Very broadly, this method consisted of analysing markets on the basis of the choices made by individual traders. Thus, the resulting theory operates at two distinct levels – that of individual choice, and that of market phenomena – even though the connection between the two levels may be provided only by an analysis of the choices of a 'representative' trader. Moreover, in order to provide a basis for a manageable analysis of market phenomena, the analysis of individual choice has to be of a particularly stereotyped and artificial kind. This method of analysis, using market theory based on choice theory of a type that allows the two levels to be connected, I will refer to as 'reductionism' on the grounds that the central idea is the *reduction* of market phenomena to (stylised) individual choices.

Considerations of tractability impose restrictions on the kind of choice theory on which the market theory can be based: the theory cannot deal with choices in all the idiosyncratic detail in which actors conceive of them, nor in terms of the elusive and wayward manner in which actors make up their minds; stable objectives and well-defined constraints are needed to provide a firm enough foundation for market theory. Just as the choice theory has to be restricted in the interests of building up to market theory, so the market theory has to be restricted in the interests of working back to choice theory. Overwhelmingly, reductionist theorising has confined its attention to situations of market equilibrium, for which situations a choice theory basis is relatively straightforward. There may, in accordance with the standard schedules, be a gap between market demand and market supply, but the choice theory from which each of these schedules is derived supposes that all choices are realisable. Accordingly, the standard schedules can tell us nothing about what will happen when the traders attempt to do what, in the aggregate, is impossible; nor are the schedules likely to persist as the traders become aware of the difficulty of doing what they had, in making their (intended) choices, regarded as straightforward. Overwhelmingly, therefore, reductionist theory has been concerned with the connection between equilibrium states of market phenomena and the choice logic from which these states could be generated. It should be noted, however, that this concern with market equilibrium is not a defining characteristic of reductionism: it is rather a way in which reductionist theorising has been rendered manageable.

2. Fundamentalism

If Keynes's ideas are to be seen as a threat to the reductionist programme, the question naturally arises of how serious a threat they are: of how fundamental the aspects are that are threatened. Those who have seen Keynes's work as a frontal assault on the whole reductionist programme, I shall refer to as 'fundamentalist Keynesians'.[1] It is the purpose of this section to exemplify such an interpretation, to consider some of the difficulties in sustaining it, and briefly to discuss its significance for economic theorising.

Like the interpretation of the work of any active mind, the interpretation of Keynes's writings requires principles of selection and emphasis: it requires a view as to what is central and what merely peripheral, what essential and what merely incidental, in his writings; in this way apparent inconsistencies and obscurities may readily be resolved, at least to the satisfaction of those adopting the interpretation. For fundamentalists, what is central and essential in Keynes's writing is to be found primarily in his article 'The general theory of employment' (1937) in the *Quarterly Journal of Economics*, an article concisely restating the argument of the *General Theory* in response to various critics; in the *General Theory* itself, the essence is said to lie in Chapter 12, 'The state of long-term expectation', and, to a lesser extent, in Chapter 17, 'The essential properties of interest and money'. The kind of considerations to be found in these places can be traced back at least to the work of ten years previously in *The End of Laissez-Faire* (1926) and, with hindsight, further back still.

An early statement of the fundamentalist position was provided by Hugh Townshend (1937). He argued that the kind of considerations raised by Keynes in his theory of liquidity preference have quite devastating consequences for reductionist price theory if they are allowed to apply to all assets. Once all prices are seen as *money* prices, and all assets as bearing a liquidity premium, price theory becomes enmeshed in the same tangle of expectational and conventional elements that characterises Keynes's theory of the rate of interest. On this view, the hope of extracting 'real' (relative) prices from their monetary context looks bleak; although, as has been argued in the previous chapter, we should not confuse Keynes's innovation in analytical procedure (in dealing with the rate of interest in association with money-holding decisions rather than with borrowing and lending) with his substantive contributions. Nevertheless, the threat to the reductionist programme does, on this view, indeed appear to be a fundamental one.

Perhaps the most uncompromising, and certainly the most tirelessly eloquent, exponent of fundamentalist Keynesianism is G. L. S. Shackle (1967; 1972; 1974). His own work has centred on the irreducibly creative element in human choice: its basis in constructs of the choosing mind. His appreciation of Keynes's contributions to economic theory has, accordingly centred around this same concern, and naturally sees these matters of expectation, uncertainty and ignorance – matters of the provision of knowledge-surrogates in the face of knowledge-deficiency – as of the essence. A most succinct distillation of Shackle's reading of Keynes has been provided by B. J. Loasby (1976).

One further line of thought must be mentioned in the present context: this is one that has attempted to use the fundamentalist aspect of Keynesianism as a way of clearing the ground to permit a return to a certain cluster of doctrines and concerns that are variously referred to as 'classical' (as distinct from 'neo-classical') or 'neo-Ricardian'. The object of this school, the most distinguished practitioner of which is Joan Robinson, is to produce a hybrid of Keynesianism with those aspects of Ricardo's work that were appropriated by Marx: Ricardo minus Say's law and the quantity theory of money.

Keynes's *QJE* paper of 1937 to which fundamentalists attach such great importance, is, first and foremost, an attack on the kind of choice theory that is required for the reductionist programme. As against the clearly specified and stable objectives and constraints required by reductionist theorising, Keynes emphasises the basis of choice in vague, uncertain and shifting expectations of future events and circumstances: expectations that have no firm foundation in circumstances, but that take their cues from the beliefs of others, and that will be sustained by hopes, undermined by fears and continually buffeted by 'the news'. He was drawing attention to both the importance and the elusiveness of the state of business confidence, and the way it unfolds. Keynes focused on the *conventional* element in valuation: the way in which valuations may persist to the extent that they are shared, but are thereby rendered both sustainable in the face of minor events and changes in circumstances, but also vulnerable to anything that threatens this conventional basis. In the course of a riot, for example, the moods and feelings of the rioters may be widely shared until, at a later stage, when the riot has lost its force, the moods and feeling may generally and rapidly revert to normal. The co-ordination of such crowd behaviour and its characteristic dynamics arise from the fact that the participants are taking their cues directly from one another. Reductionist choice theory as it has been developed does not shed any light on decisions involving such immediate and strong interdependence as this.

Once its choice-theoretic foundations are threatened, the whole reductionist programme is called into question; for without them the market theory would have nothing on which to stand, nothing to which it could be reduced. The concept of market equilibrium is in this way left exposed to attack. For without a clearly specified and stable basis in choice logic, the idea of market equilibrium is no longer connected to the realisability of individuals' intentions in the aggregate. This does not mean that market equilibrium cannot be rehabilitated; what it means is that the sustainability of equilibrium must depend on conditions that are confined to the level of the market. For the fundamentalist, however, Keynes's ideas require the rethinking and reconstruction of the whole body of a reductionist theory: its choice-theoretic basis and the equilibrium theory of markets that rests on it.

The objections to equilibrium theorising have been elaborated by fundamentalist Keynesians. Joan Robinson (1953–4) has shown that if the idea of equilibrium is pursued relentlessly, then as the concept becomes all-embracing it becomes paralysed by its own logic: equilibrium becomes a state of affairs that is, strictly, unapproachable: unless it already exists, there is no way of attaining it. Similarly, in the work of G. L. S. Shackle (1972), the idea of general equilibrium is shown to require the *pre-reconciliation*, one with another, of all present and future choices of all economic factors. On either grounds it would follow that the standard use of the method of comparative statics (or, better, 'comparative equilibria') to analyse the effects of changes in circumstances, is strictly unwarranted and illegitimate.[2] Of course, this line of thought would have nihilistic consequences for the entire corpus of economic theory and in particular for its applicability; in this respect, the line of thought reaches a purist and impractical conclusion that is in marked contrast to Keynes's own highly eclectic approach to economic theory.

The concept of equilibrium is accordingly seen by fundamentalists not as a useful simplification for economic theorists but as a distraction.[3] The essence of Keynes's thought is seen as the liberation from equilibrium theorising, as an escape from the restrictions that it imposes on our thinking. This, however, is not so much a matter of what Keynes said, as of what we are led to if we follow his line of thought, taking the *QJE* article as the definitive guide to the direction it was taking.

Where we are led by a line of thought depends a great deal, of course, on where we are disposed to go. Fundamentalists have, correspondingly, contributed freely of their own preoccupations in arriving at interpretations of Keynes's thought. At their most uninhibited, fundamentalist Keynesians have presented Keynes's ideas as an escape from the essential 'timelessness' of the modes of thought he attacked. More concretely, they have presented his central message regarding employment as concerning the existence of a liquid asset in a world of uncertainty, thus providing a retreat from the holding of real assets and the associated commitment to (employment-generating) production of a particular output. This theme has been much elaborated by Shackle and is concisely expounded by Loasby. In Joan Robinson's work, however, we find its place taken by a preoccupation with the heterogeneity of capital goods: the fact that individual items of the capital stock that history bequeaths to us cannot be costlessly transformed into one another, but exist in particular forms, embodying particular techniques, reflecting the superseded expectations of the past. The problems raised by the existence of liquid assets and durable, functionally specific capital assets are not, however, unrelated; the nature of capital goods means that holding them involves a kind of commitment while the nature of liquidity allows an escape from that particular commitment.

Fundamentalist Keynesianism, in seeing Keynes's ideas as a wholesale onslaught on the reductionist programme, does not see those ideas as providing a substitute for that programme. Rather it sees Keynes's own ideas as a *first step* in a thoroughgoing revision of economic theory. Accordingly, it sees what Keynes did *constructively* as merely a makeshift, an improvisation, a stop-gap. To take the constructive part of Keynes's work (in developing the consumption function, the marginal efficiency of capital schedule, etc.) as being the substance or result of 'the

Keynesian revolution' would therefore betoken a failure of nerve, a betrayal of fundamentalist principles.[4]

In order to sustain the fundamentalist interpretation, it is necessary to postulate that Keynes himself had occasional lapses. Thus, Joan Robinson (1973, p. 3) writes:

> there were moments when we had some trouble in getting Maynard to see what the point of his revolution really was, but when he came to sum it up after the book was published he got it into focus.

Here she refers, of course, to the *QJE* article of 1937. Again, she writes (1964, p. 75):

> The *General Theory* broke through the unnatural barrier and brought history and theory together again. But for theorists the descent into time has not been easy. After twenty years the awakened Princess is still dazed and groggy.
> Keynes himself was not quite steady on his feet . . .

She then goes on to refer (1964, p. 75) to Keynes's ('highly suspicious') remark about the timeless multiplier (1936, p. 122).

A major embarrassment for fundamentalists is to be found in the final chapter of the *General Theory*. Here we find Keynes arguing as follows (1936, pp. 378–9):

> if our central controls succeed in establishing an aggregate volume of output corresponding to full employment as nearly as practicable, the classical theory comes into its own from that point onwards. If we suppose the volume of output to be given i.e. to be determined by forces outside the classical school of thought, then there is no objection to be raised against the classical analysis of the manner in which private self-interest will determine what in particular is produced, in what proportions the factors are combined to produce it, and how the final product will be distributed between them.

This is abundantly clear, and in obvious conflict with the fundamentalist view of Keynes's thought being subversive of the whole classical ('reductionist') scheme. Accordingly, we find Joan Robinson writing (1964, p. 92), in connection with this passage, of the 'fallacy' that Keynes fell into, and remarking sadly that 'He was himself partly to blame for the perversion of his ideas' and that 'Keynes himself began the reconstruction of the orthodox scheme that he had shattered' (1971, p. ix).

A further embarrassment for fundamentalists is the fact that Keynes indicated quite clearly that he found nothing to object to in Hicks's distillation (1937) of the *General Theory* into the IS/LM framework, or what has come to be known as 'the income-expenditure model', quite devoid of any fundamentalist characteristics.[5] This again must be seen as some kind of momentary lapse on Keynes's part if the fundamentalist interpretation is to be sustained, at any rate if Keynes himself is to be allowed to be a fundamentalist Keynesian.

What, then, does fundamentalist Keynesianism amount to? It does not provide any sort of determinate theory or model of how the economy functions at the aggregate level; it does not enable one to make any definite predictions about the likely effects of alternative policies or circumstances. On the contrary, it is a viewpoint from which such constructions would appear as rather desperate makeshifts of transient applicability. Fundamentalist Keynesianism is concerned with the texture rather than the direction, as it were, of the economic process.

To stress the basis of all economic activity in more or less uncertain expectations is precisely to emphasise the openness and incompleteness of economic theorising and explanation. It does not itself provide any kind of fixed mechanism according to which the unfolding of events takes place; but it does show how one would set about constructing a narrative of events. It is a view about where the gaps are in the causal chains that can be identified in the economy: the points at which the economic process is susceptible to influence. We can accordingly begin to appreciate the deep ambivalence of this viewpoint towards economic policy. On the one hand, it sees potentiality for enormous leverage, the whole economic process moving in response to changing states of mind and consciousness; on the other hand the very precariousness of this vision leads very naturally to thoroughgoing scepticism about the predictability of the effects of attempts deliberately to apply leverage in pursuit of political objectives. The viewpoint in itself provides no guidance on whether the precariousness is so pervasive as to undermine the potential for political leverage. That is to say:

the wayward and unruly character of individual choices – and in particular investment decisions – is seen as an impediment to economic functioning; but the question that must be faced from a policy point of view is whether it is a greater impediment to the self-regulation of the economy than it is to the workings of discretionary fiscal and monetary policy. This would involve not just the consideration of an impediment to economic functioning, but a comparison between its inhibiting effects on alternative modes of economic regulation. More broadly, the comparison also arises between the effects of having investment decisions taken within alternative institutional frameworks, giving various powers and responsibilities to agencies of the state, whose regulative capacities then also become a part of the appropriate comparison.

In summary, we can say that fundamentalist Keynesians are united in seeing Keynesian ideas as posing a threat to the whole reductionist programme; and that their primary concern has been to reinforce this threat with further threats. When it comes to providing an alternative to the reductionist programme, however, matters are less unified. There is a marked contrast, for example, between the prospectus offered by Joan Robinson for the completion of the Keynesian revolution, and the insight offered by Shackle into its integrity and essence. When we move from the critical to the constructive aspects of fundamentalism, not only are matters less unified, they are also less definite. In Loasby's work, this indefiniteness is transformed into a methodological principle (1976, p. 167):

> If one can summarise in one sentence the theory of employment set forth by Keynes in his *QJE* article of 1937, it is this: unemployment in a market economy is the result of ignorance too great to be borne. The fully-specified macroeconomic models miss the point – which is precisely that no model of this situation can be fully specified.

3. Hydraulicism

During the 1940s and 1950s, there appeared a number of expositions of 'Keynesian economics', attempting to make the ideas accessible to students, and even to intelligent laymen.

What these works had in common, quite apart from matters of substance, was an unmistakable enthusiasm for (what were taken to be) Keynes's ideas. This enthusiasm was at times so unrestrained that it verged on excitement; it was the authors of these works who spoke without reservation of a 'Keynesian revolution'. It is some indication of the level of enthusiasm reached by these expositors and popularisers that one of them, Jan Pen, could write a book setting out and discussing a particular specification of a static 'Keynesian' model of relationships between a small number of macroeconomic aggregates, and give it the title *Modern Economics* (1965).

The period of Keynesian enthusiasm was really the post-war period: the ideas went cantering briskly through the 1950s and early 1960s; faltered sometime in the middle 1960s and stumbled into the 1970s.[6] More recently, this enthusiasm has become a far more partisan matter: the decade from the early 1970s to the present time was one in which there was such turmoil both at the level of economic events and at the level of the interpretation of those events, that Keynesian ideas have become a great deal more contentious that they had previously been. Accordingly, it is possible, at the present time, for a reasonable and well-informed person to believe either that Keynesian ideas have been discredited beyond any hope of rescue, or alternatively, that they have re-emerged strengthened from the ruins of monetarist-inspired experiments. This, at any rate, is the picture as it emerges at the level of popular influence, at the level of widely and influentially-held views on macroeconomic policy; at the level, that is, of Keynesianism as a doctrine about how a largely decentralised economy may be subject to broad (as opposed to detailed) central control or influence through the instrument of the budget. It is tempting to adopt the practice of referring to this doctrine as 'fiscalism' to show that it is a particular variant (and perhaps a corruption or vulgarisation) of Keynes's ideas. At any rate, it is important to keep distinct the ups and downs of Keynesianism as a policy doctrine from those of Keynesianism as an academically respectable theory of the functioning of a capitalist economy at the aggregate level. Indeed the esteem in which the two aspects have been held has tended to move in opposite directions, the period when 'fiscalist' policy enthusiasm was at its height being a time at which the intellectual interest in the underlying theory had become moribund. Again, the demise of 'fiscalism' in the late 1960s and early 1970s was accompanied by a re-awakening of interest in the underlying theoretical conceptions. (We shall have more to say about this revival in the next section of this chapter.)[7]

All this should not be allowed to give the impression, which would be quite mistaken, that the fiscal enthusiasm stemming from Keynes's ideas did not include, or could not provide, a theory in support of its policy doctrine. It could and it did. What, then, we are led to ask, is the theoretical basis for fiscal enthusiasm? How is it to be characterised as one of the strands in the development of Keynesian thought? It is to these questions that we now turn.

The theoretical content of the body of ideas that has been propagated through the educational system in the West since the Second World War as 'Keynesian Economics' (by, for example, Samuelson's pedagogically authoritative textbook) I shall refer to as 'hydraulic Keynesianism'. This designation reflects the view that the natural and obvious way to regard elementary textbook Keynesianism is as conceiving of the economy at the aggregate level in terms of disembodied and homogeneous flows. Of course, conceiving of the macroeconomy in this way will be fruitful only to the extent that there exist stable relationships between these overall flows. It is my contention that the central characteristic of 'hydraulic Keynesianism' is the belief that such stable relationships do exist at the aggregate level. It is this belief which gives some point to the hydraulic conception; without such a belief the conception would simply be a matter of national income accounting, not of economic theory.

It should be noted that the flows involved in this conception are flows of expenditure, income or output. That is to say, neither prices nor quantities per period make a separate appearance: they appear inextricably in the contribution each makes to the overall flows of spending and receipts. It should now be apparent why the belief in the existence of, and the attempt to establish, stable relationships between the overall flows is radically inconsistent with reductionism. For any reductionist programme must give a crucial role in its theorising to *prices as such* (not to the contribution they make to overall spending flows). The grounds for this are that it is prices as such which provide the incentives that individuals face in making the choices on which the whole scheme is to rest. This does not mean that hydraulic Keynesianism can allow no part at all to be played by prices; when we come to think of such prices as wage rates and interest rates we can see that this cannot be so. Correspondingly, it does not mean that reductionism is incapable of allowing overall flows to play any part in its scheme. Since these are alternative programmes for theorising, rather than alternative theories, they revolve around matters of emphasis. They do not concern what can or cannot play a part in a theory, but what can or cannot play a *central* part.

In fact, contrary to the viewpoint associated with reductionism, hydraulic Keynesianism is a scheme in which there is only one agency making deliberate acts of choice; that one agency is 'the government'. It is the belief that there are indeed stable relations among the various overall flows in the economy which provides a basis for the government to pursue its policy goals regarding the overall level of economic activity and hence, relatedly, of the level of employment. It is the stability of these aggregate relationships which provides the government with the leverage it needs to influence those flows which are not under its *direct* control. By making deliberate choices for the flows it does control (via the budget), and bearing in mind the (allegedly) stable relationships between this and the other flows which are objects of concern for economic policy, the government can, in principle, exercise an indirect control on the overall level (although not the composition) of the flows which are not the objects of anyone's deliberate choice. That is the story. On the face of it, it may appear a major triumph in the march of human reason: a dramatic and irreversible extension of the boundaries of political responsibility. Instead of unemployment and depression being seen and accepted passively, like the weather, it is to be seen as a matter for human will and design, something human agency, through the instrument of central government, could actually resist and remedy.[8] As an idea it looked both simple and good; accordingly, it was, at the end of the Second World War, rapidly assimilated to both the policy statements and the rhetoric of all major political parties.[9]

In summary, it can be seen that the hydraulic approach is in conflict with reductionist market theory. The hydraulic approach shows how things would work when market prices (and wages) will not, or will not quickly enough, or will not be allowed to, perform their allocative role; it analyses a situation in which prices are failing both as disseminators of information about relative scarcities, and in the provision of incentives to act on the basis of that information.

If the central message of the *General Theory* is that overall employment is more a matter of the demand for output than of real wages, except when 'full employment' already obtains, then that message is certainly embodied in the hydraulic approach. As such, it is an audacious simplification, which is, on the face of it, in conflict with the corpus of reductionist theorising. Furthermore, as a way of thinking about macroeconomic policy, it seems to work, to some extent, sometimes. The intellectual problem that it raises, however, is that of its own *scope*. What we need to know are the circumstances in which, and the extent to which, the operation of an economy may be conceived of in hydraulic terms. There are various approaches to this question. As we have seen in Chapter 2, a familiar one is provided by the IS/LM apparatus, within which it can be readily shown that the economy exhibits the characteristics of the hydraulic model to the extent that the interest-elasticity of expenditure is low and of the demand for money is high. With a zero interest-elasticity of expenditure and an indefinitely large interest-elasticity of demand for money, the determination of national income and output would be exactly in accordance with the hydraulic model: changes in expenditure flows would lead to changes in output flows without any repercussions on the rate of interest. In sum, it follows that the economy may exhibit the characteristics of the hydraulic model to the extent that the interest rate is impeded, for whatever reason, in its attempts to respond to changes in expenditure.

Since the IS/LM apparatus was put forward by Hicks, however, we have had something like thirty years' experience of demand management policies based on the assumption that the economy exhibits marked hydraulic characteristics in the short-run; and the question of why these policies have been less effective at some times than others naturally raises in a practical way the question of the scope of the hydraulic conception. It is therefore of considerable interest that Hicks (1974, ch. 1), in a revision of Keynesian economics in the light of this experience, does not adopt his own IS/LM apparatus for the purpose. Rather he provides, as we saw in the previous chapter, an alternative framework in which the possibility of an expansion in demand being translated into an expansion of output depends crucially on the structure of inventories at the outset of the process.

There are, of course, other approaches to the question of the scope of hydraulic theorising. Indeed, the monetarist arguments against Keynesian conclusions may be seen as one possible answer to this question: namely, that the scope of hydraulic theorising is practically non-existent. In these arguments the Keynesian conclusions are undermined by the reintroduction of a choice-theoretic basis of the standard reductionist type. As we shall see in the next section of this chapter, the work of Clower and Leijonhufvud may also be seen as contributing to this question of scope, although this is not how either of them presented his work.

4. Reconstituted reductionism

During the 1960s, there emerged a school of thought, associated primarily with the names of Clower (1969) and Leijonhufvud (1968), concerned to reappraise Keynes's contribution to economics. These writers presented their work as concerned with re-establishing and reasserting the discontinuity between Keynesian economics and its alternatives, a discontinuity that they saw as having been blurred and finally lost to view by the various activities of interpretation, condensation and reconstruction that came in the wake of the *General Theory*. This perspective has accordingly been the one within which the contribution of Clower and Leijonhufvud to our understanding of Keynes has been discussed and appraised. My purpose here, however, will be to present the dispute between, on the one hand, Clower and Leijonhufvud and, on the other, those whose views they were combating, as a family quarrel within the reductionist programme. Most fundamentally, the family quarrel is about the expendability of the concept of equilibrium: the Clower–Leijonhufvud position being that the concept of equilibrium should be abandoned in the interests of a more thorough-going reduction of Keynesian ideas to choice logic. The thesis is that once equilibrium has been abandoned and one focuses on a process of trading at disequilibrium prices, then one has a framework that is entirely congenial to Keynesian ideas, unlike the framework of equilibrium theorising which, on this view, leaves room for them in only the most attenuated and *ad hoc* form. The problem then becomes one of providing a more sophisticated specification of the constraints on individual choices, opening up the possibilities for theoretically novel and challenging forms of market interdependence arising from a schematisation of the process of disequilibrium trading.

In order to lead up to my characterisation of the work of Clower and Leijonhufvud it is appropriate to begin by discussing each writer's own characterisation of his work: how each of them conceived of the task he had set himself. I will argue that their own characterisations are in various respects unsatisfactory, and that my alternative is not therefore gratuitous.

Taking Clower first, we observe that, in the work under discussion, he advances a line of reasoning based on the idea that households re-calculate their demands for commodities in response to the experience of an inability to sell as much of their labour services as they would wish. Having advanced this 'dual-decision hypothesis' as a basis for expecting consumer spending to depend on current income, Clower goes on to speak of Keynes having had this theory of household behaviour 'at the back of his mind when he wrote the *General Theory*' (1965, p. 120). Clower goes on immediately to admit that 'I can find no direct evidence in any of his writings to show that he ever thought explicitly in these terms'. After advancing what he takes to be 'indirect evidence' for this he concludes that 'Keynes either had a dual-decision hypothesis at the back of his mind, or most of the *General Theory* is theoretical nonsense'. The picture here seems to be one of Keynes with a mind full of ideas *some* of which he got onto the pages of the *General Theory*, the task being to work out what the remainder must have been. This is a problem of reading not so much between the lines as off the edge of the page. In his conclusion, however, Clower maintains, rather more soberly, that his purpose has been 'simply to clarify the *formal basis* of the Keynesian revolution and its relation to orthodox thought' (1965, p. 124, emphasis added). This then leaves the task quite up in the air, for it is not explained how this relates to the previous concern with what Keynes had 'at the back of his mind'.

Turning to Leijonhufvud, we find that he is at some pains to try to make clear the task he has set himself. First, he makes it plain that the doctrine-historical question of 'what Keynes really said' is a strictly secondary matter for his purposes (1968, p. 9). 'The primary purpose', he explains 'remains ... to provide a fresh *perspective* from which the income-expenditure theory may be reconsidered' (1968, pp. 9–10). (The 'income-expenditure theory' is Leijonhufvud's label for the 'conceptual framework which has crystallized out of the debate triggered by the *General Theory*' (1968, p.6).) This seems straightforward enough. The difficulty arises from the fact that what was presented was not just 'Leijonhufvud's fresh perspective', but rather the fresh perspective that Leijonhufvud claimed to have distilled from the *General Theory* itself. On the face of it, the task appears to be to get a perspective on the whole debate by going back to the origins of it. But the question arises of how the responsibility for this new perspective is to be apportioned between Keynes and Leijonhufvud. Keynes may well have provided the inspiration for the task, but if the product of the distillation is to be presented as a (purified) 'Economics of Keynes' to be contrasted with the (corrupted) 'Keynesian Economics' then we are back in the realms of mind-reading, especially as this 'Economics of Keynes' can be read into the *General Theory* only with a great deal of ingenuity and determination. So although Leijonhufvud at first seems to be concerned with the rather modest task of finding *a* fresh perspective from which the development of Keynesian Economics can be surveyed or appraised, it turns out that he is in search of *the* one perspective from which the Keynesianness of these developments can be judged. What looks at first like a search for new angles turns out to be a search for authenticity.

But it is not just a matter of authenticity. For the fundamental presumption that underlies the work of Clower and Leijonhufvud is that Keynes said something important, not only for economic policy, but for economic theory. They are saying 'Let us read the *General Theory* in a search for theoretical innovation'. In other words, far from being engaged in disinterested exegesis (as the concern for authenticity might suggest) they were concerned with re-working with a view to rejuvenating (by which standards they must be judged to have had some success).

How, then, is the task that Clower and Leijonhufvud set themselves to be expressed and understood? The view I want to advance is that they were setting themselves the task of constructing a framework that would provide room or scope for Keynesian ideas. This quite rightly takes it for granted that we already have a good rough idea what Keynesian ideas are: of what the *General Theory* was driving at. What was wanted was a theoretical niche in which what were taken to be Keynes's insights could take root and thrive. The motive for this search was evidently the recognition that the framework of general equilibrium theory that had been widely adopted for attempts at precise expression of Keynesian ideas leaves practically no room or scope for them.

On its own terms, then, the essence of the Clower–Leijonhufvud position is this: that in order to accommodate Keynesian ideas we have to abandon equilibrium theorising and address ourselves to an understanding of the process of disequilibrium trading. In my terms, however, it is not just equilibrium theorising that has been shown to be uncongenial to Keynesian ideas, but rather equilibrium theorising within the reductionist programme. One can see why this should be so without even taking any detailed view about the workings of the economy. For within reductionism everything boils down to acts of choice within a well-specified system of objectives, constraints and forms of interdependence; and in equilibrium theorising we confine our attention to situations in which all the independently arrived at choices can be simultaneously realised. It then follows rather naturally, irrespective of any details of market forms or institutional arrangements, that such a system leaves no room for the 'unintended' and 'involuntary': for malfunctioning and disorder. It follows, however, from my characterisation of such theorising that there are two distinct possibilities for the accommodation of Keynesian ideas: (1) the abandonment of equilibrium; and (2) the abandonment of reductionism. Clower and Leijonhufvud consider only the former possibility. We can see, however, that the claim that equilibrium theorising *must* be abandoned in order to accommodate Keynesian ideas would require that it be established that theorising *must* be carried out in accordance with the reductionist programme.

The whole question of whether Keynesian ideas should be accommodated by abandoning equilibrium theorising rather naturally raises the question of what use Keynes himself made of the concept of equilibrium.[10] It is certainly true that Keynes made use of the term 'equilibrium'. But before we conclude that if Keynes could express his ideas in these terms then they must be perfectly compatible with equilibrium theorising, we must pause to consider the meaning of equilibrium and the uses to which an equilibrium concept might be put. We must bear in mind that it is entirely in keeping with Keynes's eclecticism that his use of the term 'equilibrium' could have been a rather desperate improvisation at one stage in the 'long struggle of escape'.

An equilibrium is a configuration which, once attained, will be maintained provided the underlying circumstances (formally, the parameters and exogenous variables) remain unchanged. Accordingly, the interest and usefulness of an equilibrium construction, as an end in itself, depends on a question which is, in principle, an empirical one, namely: What is the range of variability of the underlying circumstances over the order of magnitude of the time involved in the adjustment (near enough) to its equilibrium configurations?[11] That is to say, if the underlying circumstances are fairly stable relative to the speed of adjustment of the endogenous variables, the equilibrium configuration of the system becomes a matter of some interest in itself, and may provide a reasonably useful substitute for becoming involved in the complexities of the adjustment process. It is something to know where we are heading, provided we have some grounds for believing that we will get most of the way there before we start heading somewhere else.

It is in the light of these considerations that we can say why Keynes's use of equilibrium constructions was a peculiar one: he was concerned to discuss, among other things, the instability of the underlying circumstances of his construction. That is, one of his focuses of interest was precisely the failure of his equilibrium construction to satisfy the conditions for the routine usefulness of an equilibrium construction. Therefore, in arriving at an appreciation of Keynes's method, it is not enough to ask the nature of his construction; we must enquire also into its mode of *animation*. When we have reason to expect relatively stable underlying circumstances, the construction may be animated according to the method of comparative statics. When the animation is endemic, when one is concerned, as it were, with the restlessness of the underlying circumstances, the use of the construction becomes less straightforward, and certainly less mechanical. Whether, in this case, there is anything much left of the concept of equilibrium is a matter of no particular importance. What is important is to see that, just as one does not expect to quell a riot by taking a photograph of it, neither did Keynes's makeshift use of the equilibrium concept involve the expectation that he could freeze the economy in a particular state. Shackle has expressed this idea with characteristic elegance (1967, p. 182):

> At each curtain rise, the *General Theory* shows us, not the dramatic moment of inevitable action, but a tableau of posed figures. It is only after the curtain has descended again that we hear the clatter of violent scene-shifting.

We have seen that Clower and Leijonhufvud's version of Keynesianism is a reconstituted reductionism: it addresses itself not to the state of equilibrium but the the problem of attaining it.[12] It asks the question how a decentralised market economy might, with some degree of effectiveness, perform the task that the Walrasian auctioneer would perform smoothly. To ask this question one needs a construction in which prices adjust less than instantaneously to economic circumstances, so that at any point in time the prices may be effectively providing incentives to act, but the information they reflect will not be appropriate for the equilibrium that is being approached.

Now it may well be that formulating this question raises some of the most profound questions in macro- and monetary economics; but we are still in need, for the practical deployment of Keynesian ideas, of a usable simplification such as the hydraulic approach provides. The use of such a simplification will require an awareness of the circumstances under which it may be expected to work tolerably well: an awareness of its *scope*. This is where a reconstituted reductionism may play a part. For in order to examine the scope of a theory in which prices fail altogether to play their (ideal) allocative role, one needs a theory in which there is a *partial* failure in this respect. This latter theory could then be used to interpret the practical successes and failures of the hydraulic approach: as a way of trying to distinguish the circumstances conducive to its being an adequate simplification. Accordingly, we should see Leijonhufvud's book as not so much about the economics of Keynes as about the *scope* of the economics of Keynes. Clower and Leijonhufvud claim to have shown that, in effect, Keynes was trying to adapt the reductionist method to the expression of his own ideas by refocusing it on situations of market disequilibrium. But in displaying the analytical unmanageability of such a programme, they make it clear that, in so far as Keynes was able to come to any definite conclusions about economic functioning, he must have short-circuited such problems.

Within the hydraulic approach, employment problems are quite distinct from allocation problems; they arise at the aggregate level, and they are independent of relative prices and the composition of demand or output. The thrust of the reconstituted reductionist approach, however, is to present unemployment as a by-product or even a species of allocation problem. But if this formulation does not set any definite limits on the scope of the hydraulic simplification; all it can suggest is a general scepticism regarding the appropriateness of aggregate tools for dealing with problems that are seen as involving the internal composition of those aggregates; this, however, adds nothing to what we already know, namely that the hydraulic approach *is* a simplification and abstracts from allocation problems. The question that still remains is essentially a question of the type discussed in Chapter 2: a question of *decomposability*. It is the question of the separability of employment problems from the allocation problems on which they are, in practice, superimposed. To what extent may we disregard the allocative structure of macroeconomic aggregates? Just how blunt an instrument is demand management? If the reconstituted reductionist approach could be made tractable without collapsing into the monetarist simplification, it could be expected to shed some light on these matters (as indeed the monetarist simplification itself has done).

5. Concluding remarks

In this chapter we have considered three varieties of Keynesianism: the fundamentalist, the hydraulic and the reconstituted reductionist approaches. Each one has been located in relation to the reductionist programme: the fundamentalist approach by its rejection of the choice theory that is essential to and the (equilibrium) market theory that is typical of reductionist theorising; the hydraulic approach by its short-circuiting of reductionist market theory and its eschewal of formal choice theory foundations; and the reconstituted reductionist approach by its attempt to make room for Keynesian ideas within the reductionist programme by refocusing the market theory on disequilibrium states whilst retaining the standard choice-theoretic foundations. It remains only to make some comments on the relationship of the approaches to one another; the thrust of these comments will be that the various approaches are, in their contribution to understanding, largely complementary.

The fundamentalist approach provides a very general critique of the methods of reductionism both as regards its style of choice theory and the equilibrium theory of markets with which it is typically associated. As such, it clears the ground for the introduction of Keynesian ideas; at the same time it forms a kind of back-drop in the context of which hydraulic thinking can thrive, and, as it turns out, reductionism can reappear in a modified form. Hydraulic thinking can thrive because, in the absence of standard reductionist results, one needs some drastic simplification in order to say anything at all definite regarding forecasting or policy. (The alternative candidate is the drastic simplification provided by the quantity theory of money and its modern variants.) Reductionism can then reappear because, in making use of a drastic simplification, one is led to ask questions about its scope and limits; these questions will concern why the economy may not work in the way that standard reductionist theory indicates, and are questions that could be formulated in a modified and expanded reductionist framework.

Thus, the fundamentalist approach clears the ground for Keynesian ideas, the hydraulic approach provides the dangerous simplification that makes them at all definite and manageable, and a loosened reductionism provides the reservations and qualifications that provide guidance on the scope of this simplification. The matter may be expressed cryptically in terms of Keynes's 'long struggle of escape'. We may say that what he escaped *from* was (unreconstituted) reductionism; what he escaped *to* was the hydraulic approach; and what he went through in the process of struggle has been preserved in the fundamentalist approach. For a generation brought up on

Keynesian ideas, however, a sense of intellectual liberation is far more likely in the struggle of escape from hydraulic thinking into a reconstituted form of reductionism. In treading this particular path, Clower and Leijonhufvud were quite right to identify their work with that of Keynes; they differ from him only in their direction of travel.

Notes to Chapter 6

1. I am indebted to Don Patinkin for pointing out to me the respect in which my term 'fundamentalist' is unsatisfactory. I use the term 'fundamentalist' to signify the concern to those involved to refer to 'the texts' (of Keynes's own writings) themselves, as opposed to the secondary material of textbooks and 'the income-expenditure model', but Patinkin has pointed out that those for whom this concern is characteristic typically use these texts in a highly selective manner, and, in effect, make them the springboard for what are in reality their own ideas; these latter tendencies, as Patinkin rightly insists, do not betoken a 'fundamentalist' concern for the authority of 'the texts', but rather the very opposite. My only reason for continuing to use this term is that I have been unable to think of a better one.

2. This argument is elaborated in Coddington (1975) and Loasby (1976, ch. 3).

3. Thus: 'The argument stops when ... the equilibrium lullaby hushes further enquiry' (Robinson, 1964, p. 80). But this soporific effect is never reconciled with the concurrently held view that: 'The concept of equilibrium, of course, is an indispensable tool of analysis' (Robinson, 1964, p. 78).

4. An immediate difficulty for fundamentalists is the fact that the *QJE* article of 1937, after having advanced the arguments already discussed, goes on to stress the importance of the consumption function, which is then deployed (anticipating terminology I will introduce at a later stage) in a thoroughly hydraulic fashion.

5. See Keynes's letter of 31 March 1937 to Hicks (Hicks, 1973, pp. 9–10).

6. For an attempt at intellectual stock-taking at that time, see my 'Rethinking economic policy' (Coddington, 1974b).

7. Reflecting on the fragmentation of Keynesian thought, Leijonhufvud makes the following observation:

> For some time now, contentment with this state of the arts has rested on the motto 'The Theoretically Trivial is the Practically Important and the Practically Important is the Theoretically Trivial'. It is a disturbing formula which can hardly be a permanent basis for the further development of the field. (Leijonhufvud, 1968.)

8. This changed attitude did not come easily or quickly, and fundamental attitudes had been undergoing a process of erosion for some decades by the time Keynes came on the scene. For a painstaking documentation of this process in Britain, see Harris (1972).

9. The major bridge in Britain between Keynesian doctrines and political platforms was Beveridge (1944). The ideas were given official recognition in the White Paper *Employment Policy* (1944).

10. For a detailed exegesis of this point see Patinkin (1976, pp. 113–19).

11. We are here avoiding the large question of whether the system may approach an equilibrium configuration without shifting the equilibrium that is being approached.

12. In order to do this, Clower and Leijonhufvud avoid Joan Robinson's ultra-strict logic of equilibrium according to which the equilibrium state is unapproachable and hence the problem of attaining it, insoluble.

7

Conclusion

The preceding chapters have been concerned to follow a chain
of argument and analysis that starts from the possibility of a
link between, on the one hand, the state of the public finances,
and, on the other, the degree of capacity utilization in the whole
economy. This line of thought was pursued through the concept
of a 'Keynesian dichotomy' which provided the analytical basis
for this link, and thereby on to the concept of 'demand
deficiency' which emerges very naturally once one begins to
think about macroeconomic policy within the framework provided by such a dichotomy. Attention was then directed to
whether this aggregative notion of demand deficiency could be
given an interpretation in terms of the 'involuntary unemployment' of individuals, the provision of such an interpretation
being of especial importance from the point of view of the
diagnostic use to which the concept of demand deficiency
appears to lend itself. This concern with the rationale of demand
deficiency was then pursued in various directions. It was first
pursued, in Chapter 3, back into the cyclical context from which
it had been extracted; this then set the scene for the discussion,
in Chapter 4, of the sources of variability in expenditure
aggregates, the focus there having been the source of this
variability in the decision-making processes of individuals.

In the course of this book, I have presented the development
of Keynesian economics as a form of endeavour inspired by
pragmatic understanding and conjectures which originated
beyond the analytical grasp of its proponents; which the
development of characteristically Keynesian modes of analysis
has brought closer to our reach; but which, even now, may slip
between our fingers unless the analysis is dextrously performed.
I have presented it, that is to say, as a process of attempting to

distil the analytical residue of ideas that already exist at an intuitive, common-sense level. Within this overall endeavour there are, as we have seen, various kinds of research activity. One such form of activity is that of isolating the channels of influence (and their modes of operation) through which the Keynesian connection works; another is the search for a rationale for the Keynesian dichotomy; and there is, regardless of how these other activities progress, the large task of exploring, in a variety of contexts, the implications of the Keynesian dichotomy, and the connections that it entails. Each of these forms of endeavour could be traced into the welter of analytical activities that are to be found in the literature of the subject. The task to which Chapter 6 is addressed, however, is that of standing back to provide some kind of perspective on this whole intellectual landscape.

An acquaintance with the literature of Keynesian Economics makes it evident that the field has become most highly developed analytically where it has sought to establish what are, in effect, the *implications* of there being a Keynesian dichotomy. This is clearly manifest in the class of models within the income/expenditure framework, on which a rather extensive critical commentary already exists. This development has had its empirical counterpart in the estimation and use (for forecasting and simulation purposes) of the class of models in which, *inter alia*, the dependence of real output on aggregate expenditure is imposed as part of the model's specification. The sphere in which developments have been more meagre, however, is that in which the *rationale* for the Keynesian dichotomy (and its associated connections) has been sought. As we have argued, this literature has to be seen far more in terms of continual striving than of established results.

Although we have seen that the development of Keynesian modes of analysis may be thought of as a process of isolating and sharpening the analytical expression of connections that are already understood at the level of pragmatic insights and conjectures, it became apparent in Chapter 6 that not all of those whose work can be brought under the Keynesian label have set themselves quite the same sort of task. If we recall the three schools that were distinguished in that chapter, and think of them in relation to the Keynesian connection, we can see that their aims are certainly diverse. It could be said that whereas the hydraulic school is concerned to explore the *implications* of this connection, the reductionist school is concerned to find a *rationale* for it: that is, some more fundamental principles from which it may be derived. This way of setting the tasks, of course, makes the hydraulic school heavily dependent on the correctness of the pragmatic judgements or conjectures by means of which the Keynesian connection and its continued operation is recognised. The school is therefore in a precarious state in that, if the connection appears to falter or fail, the whole analytical edifice is threatened.

What is much less straightforward is the characterisation of the third school, the fundamentalists, in terms of their relationship to the Keynesian dichotomy. In part, I think that the fundamentalists may be distinguished by their willingness to accept the Keynesian dichotomy as a free-standing principle: a principle in its own right, not in need of 'reduction'. Yet members of this school spend a considerable amount of intellectual effort dissociating themselves from the work of the hydraulic school, in which, as has already been noted, the implications of the Keynesian dichotomy are explored. The divergence is accordingly not so much one of the *substance* of the propositions to which members of the two schools subscribe, or regard as worthy of investigation, as of the epistemological status of those propositions. Whereas the hydraulic school is prepared to allow the Keynesian connection to partake of the same status as the pragmatic judgements and conjectures from which it arose, the fundamentalists, it seems, wish to elevate it (and its associated dichotomy) to an altogether different plane of discourse: to the plane of Principles. Whatever the precise meaning of this attempted elevation may be, and however it might be justified, the motive is evident enough: it is to protect the Keynesian dichotomy from assimilation into the body of 'neo-classical economics', a body of analysis in which it is clearly felt that it would soon become submerged, to reappear only as 'special cases'. The cause for fundamentalist concern is that, even if these special cases were acknowledged to be of considerable practical importance from a policy-making viewpoint, the ideas that they embody would, once enmeshed in this way, no longer constitute a separate and distinctive vision of economic functioning and, especially, malfunctioning. Fundamentalists are distinguished, accordingly, not primarily by the propositions with which they deal, but rather by their attitude towards them. I conclude, therefore, that fundamentalism lacks intellectual autonomy, and exists only as a somewhat dissonant obbligato to the other two schools.

The emergence of the schools that I have distinguished was the result of a protracted process whereby intellectual responses to Keynesian ideas were worked out in a variety of ways. Of paramount importance as a reference point relative to which those involved in this endeavour located themselves was (and still is) the work of Sir John Hicks. I have, accordingly, reserved this work for separate treatment, in Chapter 5, as an intellectual landmark in its own right, rather than attempting to fit it into any particular school.

The conclusion that emerges from my discussion of Hicks's role in these developments is in marked contrast to that offered by those who wish to cast him in the role of 'Keynesian counter-revolutionary'; indeed, I have come to find the whole metaphor of 'revolution' thoroughly unhelpful. Apart from the crude melodramatic overtones with which it is imbued, it insinuates a wholly question-begging notion of widespread upheaval and abrupt discontinuity which, from the point of view of intellectual history, needs to be established, not applied gratuitously as a tint on the lenses through which one looks at it. Indeed, the fact that, as we have seen, Hicks displayed a deep ambivalence towards Keynes's work, should have made it evident that he lacked the simple fervour of a determined counter-revolutionary. In contrast to the imagery of political violence, however, I have come to see Hicks' role in terms which may be expressed as follows, notwithstanding their physiological implausibility. I see Keynesian economics as having been born a spineless creature, but, in its early infancy, provided by Hicks (and, of course, by those whose work his own had instigated or epitomised) with a backbone: a backbone without which it could not have survived except through the devoted attention of its closest kinsfolk. These kinsfolk, however, have such an emotional attachment to the memory of the poor helpless creature – that they thought that they alone could nurture – that they refuse to recognise the implant, and continue to bemoan the vulnerability of what, in their eyes, is still an infant, still in need of care and protection; although, in some moods, they do speak darkly of the terror he could have become, and would, perhaps, still become, if only *their* sort of backbone could be implanted.

From the point of view of macroeconomic policy, the most important conclusion that has emerged is one that was reached in Chapter 3. It concerns the danger that Keynesian analysis taken overall – as a way not only of diagnosing problems and recommending policies, but also of interpreting the reasons for their effectiveness or lack of it – may become, in effect, circular and tautologous. It is possible, that is to say, that it may be used in such a way that it appears to be vindicated, no matter what actually happens. Thus, we have seen how, according to the Keynesian dichotomy, output fluctuations are related primarily to expenditure fluctuations. If, however, it were to be found that aggregate expenditure changes have led to changes in the price level rather than to changes in real output, this need not be seen as a counter-example to Keynesian *theory*, but rather as a problem in the development of Keynesian *policies*. The impact of aggregate expenditure changes on the price level may be presented, that is to say, not as counter-examples to the principle of the Keynesian dichotomy, but rather as *vindications* of the principle of 'instrument deficiency': namely, the principle that Keynesian aggregate-demand policies may work satisfactorily only as part of a wider, more ambitious assembly of policies; and, therefore, that the very effectiveness of these policies depends on a willingness to extend their scope in response to difficulties, as and when they are encountered, in the operation of the Keynesian connection. This line of argument, however, leaves the status of the Keynesian dichotomy thoroughly obscure: is it, finally, a statement about how the economy functions, or about how the economy can be *made* to function, given a sufficiently far-reaching assembly of powers to modify its working? To the extent that the principle of instrument deficiency is always available to rationalise any apparent failures in the application of Keynesian theory, the empirical content of the theory is left in some doubt. Does it not say, in effect, that the economy will behave in a certain way, provided only that it is compelled to do so?

In order to answer this question, one would have to enquire into the way in which the policies pursued by governments – and also the compromises adopted by them between the policies they would wish to pursue and the ones that they find themselves

120   Keynesian Economics

able to pursue – have been guided by Keynesian principles of economic analysis. The analysis itself provides only an expression of a disposition of thought; where a disposition leads will depend on the opportunities presented and the obstacles encountered. The questions raised in the previous paragraph are therefore offered, not as ones which could be answered within the present work, but rather as the questions that should, in the light of this work, be addressed in the realm of applications, and, in particular, in the realm of the analysis and appraisal of macroeconomic policies. What, I believe, does follow from this work independently of such inquiries, however, is that Keynesian methods of analysis do not reveal any characteristic *technique* of policy, but rather a principle governing the aspirations that should be set for its *scope*.

This idea may be made more vivid by an analogy. Suppose one were interested in a technique for learning to swim. The Keynesian technique would contain, as one of its instructions, the principle: 'If ever one of your feet touches the bottom, move into deeper water.' As may be readily appreciated, such a principle does not itself help at all with the question of *how* exactly one may expect to swim (rather than flounder); but it does, most decidedly, impose a procedure which, if adhered to, would make the acquisition of this skill a matter of the greatest urgency. Of course, if this instruction were the only consideration, and were not overridden by a conflicting instinct for self-preservation, it would follow that all those who obeyed the instruction would, by now, have succeeded either in learning to swim, or in drowning themselves. In practice, however, a government sensing that its Keynesian policies are taking it out of its depth may, rather than plunging on anyway, flounder back towards the shallow end. (It may be able to save its face later by claiming that it was dragged back into the shallows by a life-guard from the IMF.)

What follows from all this is that the march of events is very unlikely ever clearly either to vindicate or to discredit the Keynesian approach: the same episode which, to some, appears as 'almost drowning', would appear to those with a disposition, no matter what, to keep their aspirations up, as 'almost swimming'. Indeed, within the sphere of macroeconomic policy, the issue will be even more contentious than the analogy suggests: for we lack any clear criterion that would allow us to recognise whether or not the macroeconomic analogy of 'learning to swim' has been achieved. No matter how many times one has been rescued, one may still, with the return of a modicum of bravado, turn around and abuse the life-guard for his interference.

Bibliography

Bailey, M. J., *National Income and the Price Level*, (New York: McGraw-Hill, 1962).

Barro, R. J., 'Second thoughts on Keynesian Economics', *American Economic Review*, vol. 67, no. 2 (1979), pp. 54–9.

Beveridge, W. H., *Full Employment in a Free Society*, (London: Allen and Unwin, 1944).

Blinder, A. S., 'What's "New" and What's "Keynesian" in the "New Cambridge" Keynesianism?' in K. Brunner and A. H. Meltzer (eds), *Public Policies in Open Economies*, (Amsterdam: North-Holland, 1978).

Brittan, S., 'Full employment policy: a reappraisal' in G. D. N. Worswick (ed.), *The Concept and Measurement of Involuntary Unemployment*, (London: Allen and Unwin, 1976), pp. 249–78.

Brunner, K., 'The monetarist view of Keynesian ideas', *Lloyds Bank Review*, no. 102 (1971), pp. 35–49.

Clower, R. W., 'The Keynesian counterrevolution: a theoretical appraisal' in F. H. Hahn and F. P. R. Brechling (eds), *The Theory of Interest Rates*, (London: Macmillan, 1965), pp. 103–25.

Coddington, A., 'Economists and policy', *National Westminster Bank Quarterly Review*, (February 1973), pp. 59–68.

Coddington, A., 'Creaking semaphore and beyond: a consideration of Shackle's "Epistemics and Economics" ', *British Journal for the Philosophy of Science*, vol. 26 (1974a), pp. 151–63.

Coddington, A., 'Re-thinking economic policy', *Political Quarterly*, vol. 45, no. 4 (October-December 1974b), pp. 426–38.

Coddington, A., 'What *did* Keynes really mean?', *Challenge: the magazine of economic affairs*, vol. 17, no. 5 (November-December 1974c), pp. 13–19.

Coddington, A., *Varieties of Keynesianism*, Thames Papers in Political Economy (London: Thames Polytechnic, 1976a).

Coddington, A., 'Utilitarianism today', *Political Theory*, vol. 4, no. 2 (May 1976b), pp. 213–26.

Coddington, A., 'Keynesian economics: the search for first principles', *Journal of Economic Literature*, vol. 14, no. 4 (December 1976c), pp. 1258–73.

Coddington, A., 'E. Malinvaud, "The theory of unemployment reconsidered" ' (review article), *Journal of Economic Literature*, vol. XVI (September 1978), pp. 1012–18.

Coddington, A., 'Hicks' contribution to Keynesian Economics', *Journal of Economic Literature*, vol. XVII (September 1979), pp. 970–88.

Coddington, A., 'Hanging on in difficult times', BBC Radio 3, (26 January 1980), reprinted (in abridged form) in *The Listener* (31 January 1980).

Coddington, A., 'The Economy-sized budget', BBC Radio 3, (21 February 1981), reprinted in *The Listener* (26 February 1981).

Coddington, A., 'Deficient foresight: A troublesome theme in Keynesian Economics', *American Economic Review*, vol. 72, no. 2 (June 1982), pp. 480–7.

Coutts, K., Godley, W. and Nordhaus, W., *Industrial Pricing in the United Kingdom*, (Cambridge: Cambridge University Press, 1978).

Davidson, P., *Money and the Real World*, (London: Macmillan, 1972).

Davidson, P., 'Post-Keynes monetary theory and inflation', in S. Weintraub (ed.), *Modern Economic Thought*, (Philadelphia: University of Pennsylvania Press, 1977).

Dillard, D., *The Economics of J. M. Keynes*, (London: Crosby Lockwood, 1958).

Eichner, A. S., *A Guide to Post-Keynesian Economics*, (London: Macmillan, 1979).

Fisher, M. R., 'Professor Hicks and the Keynesians', *Economica*, vol. 43, no. 171 (August 1976), pp.305–14.

Godley, W. A. H., 'Costs, prices and demand in the short run', in M. J. C. Surrey (ed.), *Macroeconomic Themes*, (London: Oxford University Press, 1976), pp. 306–9.

Haavelmo, T., 'The notion of involuntary economic decisions', *Econometrica*, vol. 18, no. 1 (1950), pp. 1–8.

Hall, R. E., 'Comment' in S. Fischer (ed.), *Rational Expectations and Economic Policy*, (Chicago: The University of Chicago Press, 1980), pp. 235–8.

Harris, J., *Unemployment and Politics*, (Oxford: Clarendon Press, 1972).

Harris, L., 'Professor Hicks and the foundations of monetary economics', *Economica*, vol. 36, no. 142 (May 1969), pp. 196–208.

Hicks, J. R., 'Mr. Keynes' theory of employment', *Economic Journal*, vol. 46, no. 182 (June 1936) pp. 238–53.

Hicks, J. R., 'Mr. Keynes and the "Classics": a suggested interpretation', *Econometrica*, vol. 5, no. 2 (1937), pp. 147–59.

Hicks, J. R., 'The monetary theory of D. H. Robertson', *Economica*, vol. 9, no. 33 (February 1942), pp. 53–7.

Hicks, J. R., *Value and Capital*, 2nd edn, (Oxford: Clarendon Press, 1946).

Hicks, J. R., *A Contribution to the Theory of the Trade Cycle*, (Oxford: Clarendon Press, 1950).

Hicks, J. R., 'Liquidity', *Economic Journal*, vol. 72, no. 288 (December 1962), pp. 787–802.

Hicks, J. R., *Capital and Growth*, (Oxford: Clarendon Press, 1965).

Hicks, J. R., *Critical Essays in Monetary Theory*, (Oxford: Clarendon Press, 1967a).

Hicks, J. R., 'The two triads', in his *Critical Essays in Monetary Theory*, (Oxford: Clarendon Press, 1967b).

Hicks, J. R., 'The "Classics" again' in his *Critical Essays in Monetary Theory*, (Oxford: Clarendon Press, 1967c).

Hicks, J. R., 'Monetary theory and history – an attempt at perspective', in his *Critical Essays in Monetary Theory*, (Oxford: Clarendon Press, 1967d).

Hicks, J. R., 'Automatists, Hawtreyans, and Keynesians', *Journal of Money, Credit and Banking*, vol. 1, no. 3 (August 1969), pp. 307–17.

Hicks, J. R., 'Recollections and documents', *Economica*, vol. 40, no. 1 (February 1973), pp. 2–11.

Hicks, J. R., *The Crisis in Keynesian Economics*, (Oxford: Basil Blackwell, 1974).

Hicks, J. R., 'Some questions of time in economics', in A. M. Tang, F. M. Westfield and J. S. Worley (eds.), *Evolution, Welfare and Time in Economics: Essays in Honour of Georgescu-Roegen* (Lexington: Lexington Books, 1976).

Hicks, J. R., *Economic Perspectives*, (Oxford: Clarendon Press, 1977).

Hill, M. J., 'Can we distinguish voluntary from involuntary unemployment?' in G. D. N. Worswick (ed.), *The Concept and Measurement of Involuntary Unemployment*, (London: Allen & Unwin, 1976), pp. 168–84.

HMSO, *Employment Policy*, (London: Cmd. 6527, May 1944).

Johnson, H. G., '*The General Theory* after twenty-five years', *American Economic Review*, vol. 51, no. 2 (May 1961), pp. 1–17.

Johnson, H. G., 'Monetary theory and policy' in *Surveys of Economic Theory*, vol. I, prepared for the American Economic Association and the Royal Economic Society (London: Macmillan, 1965), pp. 1–45.

Kahn, R. F., 'The relation of home investment to unemployment', *Economic Journal*, vol. 41 (June 1931), pp. 173–98.

Kahn, R. F., 'Unemployment as seen by the Keynesians' in G. D. N. Worswick (ed.), *The Concept and Measurement of Involuntary Unemployment*, (London: Allen & Unwin, 1976), pp. 19–34.

Keynes, J. M., 'A Treatise on Probability' (1921), as reprinted in Keynes's *Collected Writings*, Vol. VIII (London: Macmillan, for the Royal Economic Society, 1973).

Keynes, J. M., *The End of Laissez-Faire*, (London: The Hogarth Press, 1926).

Keynes, J. M., *The General Theory of Employment, Interest and Money*, (1936), as reprinted in Keynes's *Collected Writings*, Vol. VII (London: Macmillan, for the Royal Economic Society, 1973).

Keynes, J. M., 'The general theory of employment', *Quarterly Journal of Economics*, vol. 51, no. 2 (February 1937), pp. 209–23.

Keynes, J. M., *The Collected Writings of John Maynard Keynes*, Vol. XIII, ed. D. Moggridge (London: Macmillan, for the Royal Economic Society, 1973).

Keynes, J. M., *The Collected Writings of John Maynard Keynes*, Vol. XIV, ed. D. Moggridge (London: Macmillan, for the Royal Economic Society, 1973).

Kregel, J. A., *The Reconstruction of Political Economy*, (London: Macmillan, 1973).

Laidler, D. E. W., *The Demand for Money: Theories and Evidence*, 2nd edn, (New York: Dun-Donnelly, 1977).

Lakatos, I., 'Falsification and the Methodology of Scientific Research Programmes', in I. Lakatos and A. Musgrave (eds), *Criticism and the Growth of Knowledge*, (Cambridge: Cambridge University Press, 1970).

Leijonhufvud, A., *On Keynesian Economics and the Economics of Keynes*, (New York: Oxford University Press, 1968).

Leijonhufvud, A., 'Effective demand failures', *Swedish Journal of Economics*, vol. 75, no. 1, 1973, pp. 27–48.

Lipsey, R. G., 'Structural and deficient demand unemployment reconsidered', in B. J. McCormick and E. Owen Smith (eds), *The Labour Market*, (Harmondsworth: Penguin, 1968), pp. 245–65.

Loasby, B. J., *Choice, Complexity and Ignorance*, (Cambridge: Cambridge University Press, 1976).

Lucas, R. E., Jr., 'Econometric Policy Evaluation: A Critique', in K. Brunner and A. H. Meltzer (eds), *The Phillips Curve and Labour Markets*, (Amsterdam: North-Holland, 1976), pp. 19–46.

Lucas, R. E., Jr., 'Understanding business cycles' in K. Brunner and A. H. Meltzer (eds), *Stabilization of the Domestic and International Economy*, (Amsterdam: North-Holland, 1977), pp. 7–29.

Malinvaud, E., *The Theory of Unemployment Reconsidered*, (Oxford: Basil Blackwell, 1977).

Minsky, H. P., *John Maynard Keynes*, (London: Macmillan, 1976).

Minsky, H. P., 'An "Economics of Keynes" perspective on money', in S. Weintraub (ed.), *Modern Economic Thought*, (Philadelphia: University of Pennsylvania Press, 1977).

Neild, R. R., *Pricing and Employment in the Trade Cycle*, (Cambridge: Cambridge University Press, 1963).

Ohlin, B., 'Some notes on the Stockholm theory of savings and investment', *Economic Journal*, vol. 47, nos. 1 and 2 (March and June 1937), pp. 53–69, 221–40.

Patinkin, D., 'Liquidity preference and loanable funds: stock and flow analysis', *Economica*, vol. 25, no. 100 (November 1958), pp. 300–18.

Patinkin, D., *Money, Interest, and Prices*, 2nd edn (New York: Harper & Row, 1965).

Patinkin, D., *Keynes' Monetary Thought*, (Durham, North Carolina: Duke University Press, 1976).

Pen, J., *Modern Economics*, (Harmondsworth: Penguin, 1965).

Perlman, M., 'The roles of money in an economy and the optimum quantity of money', *Economica*, vol. 38, no. 151 (May 1971), pp. 233–52.

Rizzo, M. J. (ed.), *Time, Uncertainty and Disequilibrium*, (Lexington: D.C. Heath, 1979).

Robertson, D. H., *A Study of Industrial Fluctuations*, (London: P. S. King, 1915).

Robertson, D. H., 'Mr. Keynes and the Rate of Interest', in *His Essays in Monetary Theory*, (London: P. S. King, 1940).

Robertson, D. H., 'Some notes on the theory of interest', in *His Essays in Money and Interest*, (London: Fontana, 1966).

Robinson, J., 'The production function and the theory of capital', *Review of Economic Studies*, vol. 21, no. 2 (1953–4), pp. 81–106.

Robinson, J., *Economic Philosophy*, (Harmondsworth: Penguin, 1964).

Robinson, J., *Economic Heresies*, (London: Macmillan, 1971).

Robinson, J., 'What has become of the Keynesian revolution?' in J. Robinson (ed.), *After Keynes*, (Oxford: Basil Blackwell, 1973), pp. 1–11.

Samuelson, P. A. and Solow, R., 'Analytical aspects of anti-inflation policy', *American Economic Review*, vol. 50, no. 2 (1960), pp. 177–94.

126 KEYNESIAN ECONOMICS

Shackle, G. L. S., *The Years of High Theory*, (Cambridge: Cambridge University Press, 1967).
Shackle, G. L. S., *Epistemics and Economics*, (Cambridge: Cambridge University Press, 1972).
Shackle, G. L. S., 'Keynes and today's establishment in economic theory: a view', *Journal of Economic Literature*, vol. 11 (June 1973), pp. 516–519.
Shackle, G. L. S., *Keynesian Kaleidics*, (Edinburgh: Edinburgh University Press, 1974).
Shapiro, N., 'The revolutionary character of post-Keynesian economics', *Journal of Economic Issues*, vol. 11, no. 3, (1977), pp. 541–60.
Solow, R. M., 'On theories of unemployment', *American Economic Review*, vol. 70, no. 1 (1980a), pp. 1–11.
Solow, R. M., 'What to do (macroeconomically) when OPEC comes', in S. Fischer (ed.), *Rational Expectations and Economic Policy*, (Chicago: University of Chicago Press, 1980b), pp. 249–67.
Standing, G., 'The notion of voluntary unemployment', *International Labour Review*, vol. 120, no. 5 (1981), pp. 563–79.
Townshend, H., 'Liquidity-premium and the theory of value', *Economic Journal*, vol. 47, no. 1 (March 1937), pp. 157–69.
Tsiang, S. C., 'Walras' law, Say's law and liquidity preference in general equilibrium analysis', *International Economic Review*, vol. 7, no. 3 (September 1966), pp. 329–45.
Weintraub, S. (ed.), *Modern Economic Thought*, (Philadelphia: University of Pennsylvania Press, 1977).
Weintraub, S., 'Hicksian Keynesianism: Dominance and decline', in S. Weintraub (ed.), *Modern Economic Thought*, (Philadelphia: University of Pennsylvania Press, 1977).
Wootton, B., *Lament for Economics*, (London: Allen & Unwin, 1938).
Worswick, G. D. N., 'The end of demand management?', *Lloyds Bank Review*, no. 123, 1977, pp. 1–18.

INDEX

Date